THE *HELPFUL* MARRIAGE BOOK

THE *HELPFUL* MARRIAGE BOOK

Biblical Wisdom for Husbands and Wives

TIM BAYLY
WITH MARY LEE BAYLY

WARHORN MEDIA
BLOOMINGTON, INDIANA

WARHORN MEDIA
2401 S Endwright Rd.
Bloomington, IN 47403
WARHORNMEDIA.COM

© 2022 by Tim and Mary Lee Bayly. All rights reserved.

Unless otherwise indicated, all Scripture quotations are from the NEW AMERICAN STANDARD BIBLE®, © 1960, 1962, 1963, 1968, 1971, 1972, 1973, 1975, 1977, 1995 by The Lockman Foundation. Used by permission.

Printed in the United States of America

ISBN-13: 978-1-940017-42-6 (paperback)
ISBN-13: 978-1-940017-43-3 (PDF)
ISBN-13: 978-1-940017-44-0 (EPUB)
ISBN-13: 978-1-940017-45-7 (Kindle)

Cover design by Ben Crum. Typesetting and layout by Alex McNeilly. The text is set in 11/14 pt Minion 3, a typeface designed by Robert Slimbach.

*To our Heavenly Father, Who said,
"It is not good for the man to be alone."*

Contents

Acknowledgments ix

Introduction. Your Unique Marriage 3
1. Till Death 11
2. Isaac Was Comforted 18
3. Male and Female 27
4. The Best Wedding Gift 42
5. What about Birth Control? 49
6. Leaving and Cleaving 67
7. You Need the Church 77
8. Fight the Good Fight 87
9. Labor of Love 107
10. One Flesh 124
11. Raising Children 143
12. She Is Your Companion 162
Conclusion. Unless the Lord Builds the House 180

Appendix. Concerning Physical Abuse 189
Scripture Index 201

Acknowledgments

First, Mary Lee and I thank the men who once again have given themselves to editing, typesetting, formatting, and design. On this particular book, we thank our content editor, Nathan Alberson, for his jealousy over the needs of our audience. Two new copy editors, David Canfield and Joshua Congrove, did much of the preliminary work. Then, of course, faithful perfectionist Alex McNeilly gave himself to finishing the project from copyediting to layout, typesetting, and formatting for each of the platforms. We thank Jody Killingsworth for passing along the suggestion for the title, and our son-in-law Ben Crum for his cover design.

Concerning the book's content, we wish to thank those married couples who have been honest and humble, allowing us into their homes and marriages so we were able to come to understand the difficulties and joys of Christian marriage. There are many unwilling to open their homes to the intimacy of authentic Christian fellowship and hospitality, and for good reason. Every marriage is between a difficult man and a difficult woman. We thank God for those husbands and wives who demonstrated the grace of the Holy Spirit in their family life, helping us to hope for the same in our own family life. By faith, they allowed us to see their sin, which helped us have faith for our own sin being no terminal obstacle to God's work and blessing in our family life also.

Nothing compares to the beauty and Christian witness of a husband and wife living by faith in our Lord Jesus Christ. We mention, first and foremost, Peter and Sharon Taylor; also, John and Carol Dettoni, Bob and Anne Woodson, and Don and Evelyn Jerred.

Too, we wish to thank the officers and members of Trinity Reformed Church who, despite seeing our sins in technicolor, were willing to feed from our hands and mouths as we shepherded them. And yes, "we." The biblical pattern is the pastor and his wife shepherding the husbands and wives of the church.

Also, we thank those Christian men and women in our congregations who were willing to divorce their spouses as a confession of faith. Rather than appeasing their godless spouses as they trampled on their vows, they confessed their faith in marriage as God ordained it and committed themselves and their children to the safety and nurture of the Bride of Christ.

With this book, we come to our retirement from pastoral ministry. As we look back, we recognize the humility of sheep who don't demand they be shepherded by angels, but accept those sinful souls who are their inferiors and whom God is pleased to use to feed, clothe, rebuke, exhort, and encourage them as they enter the kingdom of God.

Finally, we thank our own fathers and mothers, Ken and Margaret Taylor and Joseph and Mary Lou Bayly, who loved and bore the fruit of their love in many, many children raised in the nurture and admonition of the Lord. It was never easy for them. That was clear to their children and grandchildren. Yet, as Dad put it so well in one of his final columns for *Eternity*:

> Pressures on marriage are nothing new. Don't think my generation and previous generations were free from the relational, emotional, financial, health, and spiritual problems—including the temptation to commit adultery—that confront you today. We were confronted; some of us had good marriages, some poor ones.
>
> But divorce wasn't an "out" for previous generations of Christians. Maybe that was the reason we honored our promise to stick to our mate for life, "until death us do part."
>
> I like to think that a lot of us were persuaded that we'd made the best choice in the whole world and that nobody else (including young flesh) could be better. And I like to think that we had a bit more concern for our children.[*]

Tim Bayly
January 2022

---

[*] Joe Bayly, "Who Are We to Judge?" Out of My Mind, *Eternity*, November 1982, reprinted in *Out of My Mind: The Best of Joe Bayly*, ed. Tim Bayly (Zondervan, 1993), 186–187.

THE *HELPFUL* MARRIAGE BOOK

Introduction
Your Unique Marriage

> Do not be conformed to this world, but be transformed by the renewing of your mind, so that you may prove what the will of God is, that which is good and acceptable and perfect.
>
> — Romans 12:2

Leo Tolstoy began *Anna Karenina* with one of literature's most famous opening lines: "All happy families are alike; each unhappy family is unhappy in its own way."[1]

Tolstoy was wrong. Happy families are not all alike. Each is happy in its own delightful way. It's *un*happy families that are alike.

Take Tolstoy's own family. It was very unhappy, yet not "in its own way." His family was the same as all unhappy families whose husbands and fathers are proud, selfish, and adulterous.

But each happy family is different, unique in its happiness. Each marriage is too, and the wise husband and wife will work to discover what makes their own marriage happy, without feeling pressure to copy their parents or friends.

This may feel like an obvious lesson, but it's an important one, and it's how this book must begin. Why? Because this is not a book of formulas or lists.

Most of us like to be told precisely what we should do to guarantee success, especially when it comes to marriage and parenting. We like to check things off. We like to plug in to a system, live by specific rules, and then wait for all the good results we've been promised.

Take parenting, for example. People quote the proverb,

> Train up a child in the way he should go,
> Even when he is old he will not depart from it.
>
> (Prov. 22:6)

They think, *Yes, just what we needed. Now if we can only figure out exactly what it means to train up a child in the way he should go . . .*

Fear not. There are plenty of people ready to tell you precisely what they do, how often, and when. The book *Growing Kids God's Way* comes to mind. Hundreds of thousands of young Christian couples have used this book, and others like it, hoping to apply the right formula and raise their own kids "God's way." These manuals tell parents when to wake their child, when to feed him, how long he should stay up, the proper routine to put him back to bed, and so on.

But then, reality hits. *What went wrong? Why are the kids not turning out the way they were supposed to? Why is it so hard? Why is Johnny throwing tantrums in the grocery store? Why is little Susie biting children in the nursery? We were following all the rules!*

As I write I can't stop thinking about the couple from our church who were huge proponents of *Growing Kids God's Way*. They have long since left the congregation, they're divorced, and their adult children are now, shall we say, no commendation of their parents' childrearing. After many years as a pastor, I've seen the bad fruit in the lives of adult

INTRO YOUR UNIQUE MARRIAGE

children whose parents were most confident in their childrearing techniques.

The problem with all these systems and rules is that they do not take into account the ways original sin shows up individually, and therefore uniquely, in each of our children. Nor in ourselves as fathers and mothers. Formulas and to-do lists have their place, but God did not make us drones, and He does not intend for us to live by anyone else's one-size-fits-all approach.

But if this book is not a step-by-step guide to a happier marriage, what is it? Hopefully something much more helpful. Each chapter focuses on some aspect of God's design for marriage which is under attack today, and seeks to strengthen you in your resolve to obey God's commands to husbands and wives. And then, rather than provide you with the shining image of the perfect marriage, this book will encourage *you* to find the specific ways to live out God's design in accordance with you and your spouse's own personalities. And this is what I want to double down on at the outset: *The specifics will be unique to everyone.*

This is because every happy family really is different. Think of how much our individuality matters to God: "Indeed, the very hairs of your head are all numbered" (Luke 12:7). God is the creator of diversity. He is a God of originality. He created DNA. He created the universe. And He creates each of us unique individuals. We are each utterly alone in our combination of looks, capacities, handicaps, skills, thoughts, emotions, walking patterns, likes, gifts, weaknesses, sins, and righteousness. Every mother teaches her children this truth, and although we make fun of it, it's absolutely true: each child is unique and that's so wonderful.

And just as each child is unique, so each husband and wife are unique. Each father and mother has their own way of fathering and mothering, and each son and daughter their own way of responding to their father and mother. Each family has its own particular look, sound, and even smell.

We have a grandson who could recognize families based on their smells. If you found some piece of clothing left on the floor at church, you could ask him whose it was. He would sniff it and say it belonged to the Smiths, or to the Wegeners, or to some other family. He had a great smeller and was always right. Every family has its own smell.

In the same way, every family has its own unique ways of serving the Lord. And this uniqueness is not in opposition to God's larger creation decrees. For example, God made us each either male or female, and He made the male to be the head of the home. This is called God's "creation order" and it's carefully spelled out and commanded across God's Word. Yet this order does not dictate who manages the family finances, who keeps the cars running, who spanks the children, who does the dishes, who takes out the garbage, who reads the Bible during family devotions, and so on. Some families believe headship requires the father always to be the one to read the Bible and lead prayer in family devotions. I generally don't argue with them—so long as they don't begin to tell every family in the church they should do the same.

Thirty years ago, a zealous young wife set up an appointment to talk with me. When she came in my office, she told me she'd come to confront me about Mary Lee keeping our family's checkbook. As she saw it, this betrayed my teaching on the creation order. If the husband is the head of his wife, he should be the one to write checks and balance the checkbook.

I tried to explain that while I agreed with her principle, I didn't see the necessity of her application. Mary Lee spent most of our money and therefore wrote most of our checks, so it only made sense for her to keep the checkbook. I assured

INTRO YOUR UNIQUE MARRIAGE

this young woman this didn't mean I was disengaged from our family's finances, but she still left unsatisfied.

Today, I remain firm in cautioning us in our judgments about how larger principles of manhood and womanhood apply to specific responsibilities in our homes. Such decisions should be made by the husband and wife in a way that reflects the individual strengths and weaknesses God has given each of us. Maybe this particular husband can't read, and he gives the Bible to his wife or a child, asking them to read the night's portion for family devotions. Maybe this particular wife never learned to sew, but her husband is a tailor. Maybe the husband can't count, but his wife is a CPA. We must be careful not to peer in on others' marriages, then try to make ours work the way theirs do.

Right after we were married, Mary Lee received a letter from a single friend who was a divorce attorney. He gave us this good advice:

> Above all, if [Tim] had the best features of each of the husbands of your girl friends, he would have been a Greek God, and never have married you. If you measure him by the best features of others, he will always look bad. If you measure him by the worst of others, he will always look good. If Jill's (just making up names) husband "Always helps with the dishes," remember that Jill is bragging about her husband (or her control of him). She isn't telling you about the beer cans on top of the TV, the crackers left in bed, nor the garbage he never takes out. If she is going to brag, she is only going to tell half the story. Remember that all men have good points and bad.

Now, thanks to social media, we can see what every person we ever met is doing with their home remodel, where they are spending their vacation, where their children go to school, or how well they are doing in their homeschooling. We can even peek in on their sweet and enviable anniversary dinner.

We can't help but compare our measly little apartment with their beautiful home, and we envy their ability to take annual family vacations when all we can afford is stay-cations. We look longingly at the picture of the couple celebrating their anniversary with a dinner date, unable to forget that our husband forgot our anniversary.

Picture a family sitting around the breakfast table on a Saturday morning. The table is full of eggs and bacon, fruit juice, and coffee. This breakfast was made by the husband. Wow. What's not to like about that? If you're a wife, you might be envious.

But let's go behind the scene. Believe it or not, the wife behind the camera resents her husband for making this big breakfast for the family every Saturday morning. As she explained it to us, her husband really thought *she* should make a nice big breakfast for the family every Saturday morning. Since she had no inclination to do so, he did it, but it came with his unspoken resentment toward her for not making it herself, which was then compounded by her resentment toward him for making it. So what appears, on the surface, to us to have been a lovely family breakfast, actually was not.

What a tangled web we weave.

Now, I know we said no lists, but if you'll indulge me:

Step 1: Remember that every home is unique.
Step 2: Find your own ways of obeying the commands of God.
Step 3: Don't compare yourself to other people. They are just that: other people.

INTRO YOUR UNIQUE MARRIAGE

In making comparisons, it is easy for young married people to fall into the trap of comparing their own marriage to that of their parents. In the case described above, the reason the husband thought his wife should make a big breakfast on Saturdays was because his mother had always done that when he was growing up. Whatever we grew up with is what we think is normal.

I remember one dinner we had with some newlyweds. There was tension in the air, but we didn't know why. We found out later it was because the husband was waiting for his wife to grill the meat (because his mother had always done it), while she was waiting for him to grill the meat (because her father had always done it). In the meantime, we milled around with the other guests, sensing the tension.

These unspoken expectations need to be talked about, sometimes argued about, but never ignored. In her delightful book *Sixpence in Her Shoe*, Phyllis McGinley describes her morning breakfast routine with her husband:

> Never eating breakfast together is the simple cornerstone of our marriage and my husband's bounding good health. It was not an easy rule to keep. Having been strictly brought up, I knew how every man should be sent off to work—heartily fed, heartened by soothing conversation, waved farewell to at the door.
>
> The trouble is that I am a late starter, my husband an early one....
>
> After our first few stunned matutinal encounters, with me blundering blindly about the kitchen trying to interest him in an omelet ... we came to an agreement.
>
> "Look, pet," he said firmly on the fourth morning, "Stop acting like the Ideal Wife in a soap opera. I don't *want* a domestic scene before 8 AM. I'll promise not to strike you

> with a blunt instrument if you promise not to lift that little tousled head off the pillow till I get out the back door."
>
> So for more years than I care to count, I have laid his place the night before, left a loaf near the toaster, and allowed his coffee to be barbarically heated over by himself.
>
> It still goes against my housewifely grain. But to this amicable arrangement I credit the fact that his doctor annually congratulates him on his beautiful blood pressure.[2]

Since opposites attract, we tend to marry someone very different from ourselves. If you are a morning person, no doubt you are married to a night owl. If you like to keep the house warm, no doubt your husband likes it cool. If you are a lover of the outdoors, your wife is likely to love the comforts of home.

Certainly you have examples of your own where you have had to work out family differences and personality preferences after you got married. Certainly also, your marriage will not be like that of your parents or in-laws. It's okay. You are forging new territory.

Your marriage is new, your family is new; together you are a new thing. Don't resent your wife or husband because they are not like your mother or father. Stop comparing your marriage to that of your parents, neighbors, or social media friends. Embrace the newness.

Love God, love your husband or wife, and learn to reflect the beauty of God's true diversity. Study God's commandments and then be the unique people God created you to be. Learn God's purposes for marriage and then live the unique marriage God has created through you.

CHAPTER 1
Till Death

They are no longer two, but one flesh. What therefore God has joined together, let no man separate.

— Matthew 19:6

Genesis records the history of God's work of creation. He looked at that work and declared it "good" six times. Then, finishing His work, He looked it all over and declared it "very good" (Gen. 1:31). Only one thing was *not* good: "It is not good for the man to be alone; I will make him a helper suitable for him" (Gen. 2:15).

God is perfect in everything He does, so He wasn't saying His work was defective. Just incomplete. Seeing Adam alone led God to put the finishing touch on His creation. He completed man with woman. He completed Adam with Eve. Adam needed a helper. God created Eve to be that helper. Man needed a helper, so God created woman.

If it's appropriate to have favorite parts of the Bible, I would choose Adam's response when God woke him from his sleep and introduced him to his wife:

> This is now bone of my bones,
> And flesh of my flesh;

> She shall be called Woman,
> Because she was taken out of Man.   (Gen. 2:23)

We don't have any record of wedding vows between Adam and Eve, but from this moment they were man and wife. God made them so, and you can feel Adam's joy. This is the first love song in history.

This exclamation by Adam is a perfect statement for every marriage. The pastor says, "I now declare you man and wife. What God has joined together, let no man divide." And every man since Adam shares his joy, "This is now bone of my bones, and flesh of my flesh." All the waiting is over. All the yearning. All the incompleteness and aloneness. The bridegroom finally has his bride, a helper who loves him and will stay by his side until death separates them.

Not long ago, I spoke with a friend in his eighties who lost his wife last year. I asked how he was doing. Was he lonely? He's a lawyer who doesn't like to talk about himself, and he simply responded, "It's like an amputation without anesthesia."

By God's grace, many of the readers of this book will understand something of the love that goes into a sad statement such as that one. But if all we felt about our marriages was love and romance, there wouldn't be much of a market for books like this one. Maybe you're in a particularly difficult marriage, and you think (although you would never say) that this brother's difficulty would be your dream.

It's true. When we marry, things don't stay perfect. Things didn't stay perfect for Adam and Eve either. Difficulties come as both husband and wife sin against each other. But right here, let's stop and hammer this home: *Marriage is irrevocable.*

Adam and Eve were married. They were joined together by God, and you are joined to your husband or wife in the same way. The two are one. There was no going back then, and there's no going back now. The thing is over and done. You can't take it back. G. K. Chesterton described this reality with a colorful comparison: "Posting a letter and getting married are among the few things left that are entirely romantic; for to be entirely romantic, a thing must be irrevocable."[1]

You and your spouse took vows. Keep it firmly in mind that those vows are for life, and that your wedding guests and God Himself are witnesses to those vows.

The liturgy used in most Christian weddings today has come down to us over a thousand years. At its center are the vows, unchanged for centuries. In the 1549 Book of Common Prayer, they appear as follows:

> MAN: I N. take thee N. to my wedded wife, to have and to holde from this day forwarde, for better, for wurse, for richer, for poorer, in sickenes, and in health, to love and to cherishe, til death us departe: according to Goddes holy ordeinaunce: And therto I plight thee my trouth.
>
> WOMAN: I N. take thee N. to my wedded husbande, to have and to holde from this day forwarde, for better, for woorse, for richer, for poorer, in sickenes and in health, to love, cherishe, and to obey, till death us departe: accordyng to Goddes holy ordeinaunce: And thereto I geve thee my trouth.[2]

Five and a half centuries later, the vows in many Christian wedding services sound much the same. The language has been updated, but they still always include that fateful phrase, "till death." "Till death us departe." "Till death us do part." "Till death separates us."

Why till death? Because marriage is God's holy ordinance. He made it, and it is irrevocable.

Of course, within every church and family are men and women who have never taken such vows. There's nothing wrong with staying single. This is a holy calling from God that many have followed in order to serve Him more single-mindedly, and across the ages these souls have been a gift to the church.

But those of us who are married must never think or act in a way contrary to our marriage vows. You've put your hand to the plow. Don't look back.

The most distinct memory I have from our honeymoon was waking up in the morning and looking to my right, seeing Mary Lee lying there sleeping peacefully—then thinking, "The rest of my life." It was a joy, but the weight of the thing almost overwhelmed me. I felt the heaviness of our lifelong commitment, and it was good for me to do so.

You've probably heard friends and family talking about some difficult marriage and expressing frustration that it was ever solemnized. If it was a Christian wedding, the pastor may get the blame: *He should have seen what a narcissist the man was and protected the woman from him. He should have seen how emotionally immature the woman was. They should never have married. No pastor should ever have officiated at their ceremony.*

When I hear such things, my response is always the same (whether I say it out loud or not). The thing is done. Talking about what preceded the marriage is beside the point. What's needed now is not armchair quarterbacks, but help.

When I was a young pastor, I looked up to an older pastor from Philadelphia whose name was Ben Sheldon. Ben and his wife, Amy, had been blessed by God with many children. Ben once told me a couple had just visited his congregation and introduced themselves and their family. Their children were young, and when they finished saying the children's names, the mother pointed to one of the children and commented nonchalantly to Pastor Sheldon, "She's our accident."

Ben immediately responded, "That is a *godless* thing to say. Why would you *ever* speak about one of your children God has blessed you with in such a way?"

I didn't ask Ben how they'd responded or whether he ever saw them again, but I learned an important lesson that day. Convenient or not, easy or difficult—what God has done, God has done, and we should never speak of God's actions lightly or joke about them. This goes for the children God gives us, and the marriages.

But there is another point almost as important. A vow is a vow, and God commands us to keep our vows:

> If a man makes a vow to the Lord, or takes an oath to bind himself with a binding obligation, he shall not violate his word; he shall do according to all that proceeds out of his mouth. (Num. 30:1–2)

Let's be done with talk about this or that marriage being stupid, this or that couple being mismatched. Every marriage is between sinners. Every marriage is difficult. We know it going in. As a matter of fact, this is what makes the wedding romantic.

When Mary Lee and I were preparing for our wedding ceremony, we'd asked our fathers to officiate. Although both of them worked in publishing, they'd each been ordained to pastoral ministry earlier in life, and were happy to be able to share this joyful work.

Two days before the wedding, my dad took me aside and said, "Tim, you need to promise divorce will never be an option in your marriage, or I will not perform your ceremony."

I said okay, but walked away shocked. Of course divorce would never be an option. Why was he requiring us to promise that?

Later I told Mary Lee Dad's requirement, and was discouraged (but not surprised) by her response: "Well, of course we're not planning on getting a divorce. But no one ever plans to get a divorce, and who knows what will happen?"

To which I responded, "Well, Dad said he wouldn't marry us unless we say we'll never get divorced."

Suffice it to say, many times during the conflicts and difficulties of the first ten years of our marriage, Mary Lee and I realized, and often commented on, the wisdom and blessing of Dad's requirement. Because of it, we never contemplated divorce. We never threatened separation. These days, when we describe how difficult our first years were to others, we often say if either of us had tried to leave the other, we'd have had to go to our spouse's parents, because our own parents wouldn't have let us in the door.

After recounting God's creation of woman for man, Eve for Adam, Genesis follows it up with this editorial statement: "For this reason a man shall leave his father and his mother, and be joined to his wife; and they shall become one flesh" (Gen. 2:24). You and your wife or husband are now "one flesh." You don't have to try to be. You are. The two of you have become one. You are married. This is your steady state until death.

So, well done. You're both to be commended for taking the huge step of faith today by not burning with lust and just living together, but marrying.[3]

Only the people of God are romantic today. We publicly promise never to consider divorce as an option. We promise never to have sex with anyone other than our own spouse. We promise to submit to our sinful husband. We promise to cherish our sinful wife. We promise to do these things through good times and bad, through wealth and poverty, through sickness and health.

Let's make a commitment not to whine about our marriage, our wife, or our husband. And let's acknowledge that we have—all of us—hard work to do to make ourselves easier to be married to and easier to love. Let's assume that *we* are the problem before we blame our husband or our wife. Instead of complaining and letting faithlessness own our heart, let's trust the God who has blessed us with marriage. And what God has joined together, let no man separate.

Chapter 2
Isaac Was Comforted

> Blessed be the God and Father of our Lord
> Jesus Christ, the Father of mercies and God of
> all comfort, who comforts us in all our affliction
> so that we will be able to comfort those who
> are in any affliction with the comfort with
> which we ourselves are comforted by God.
>
> — 2 Corinthians 1:3–4

It's a fad right now to write and talk about marriage being a school of sanctification. But isn't that obvious? Maybe not, if everyone's talking about it as if it's a surprise today.

If we believe in the Fall and understand its corruption of everything God created, we shouldn't be surprised at the difficulty of marriage. Of course marriage is sanctifying. Being a husband is sanctifying. Being a wife is sanctifying. Childbirth is sanctifying. Being a son or daughter is sanctifying. Being a father or mother is sanctifying. Being a sheep under the care of elders is sanctifying. Being an elder caring for sheep is sanctifying. Yes, life is hard, and carrying out the responsibilities God delegates to us makes it that way. But we all know the adage, "Nothing ventured, nothing gained."

So now, you've left the harbor and set your marriage-ship off for distant shores. Out here at sea, tossed by winds and waves, can you stop to be thankful? Will you give thanks to

ISAAC WAS COMFORTED

God who made the two of you one? May I warn you that ungrateful hearts don't find God responsive?

To believe in our Lord Jesus is to be thankful for the Father's love which sent Jesus to the cross to die for sinful people like you and me. Like your wife or husband. Like your sons and daughters. The Christian life begins with gratitude. What other response could the Christian have to God revealing that He loved the world so much that He sent His only begotten Son to the cross?

Thankfulness is not an observation of life, but an expression of faith. The just live by faith, so they exude thankfulness—which often is even more visible in the midst of their difficulties. Yes, marriage is sanctifying. But marriage is also a great blessing, and don't ever forget it. Count your blessings. Name them one by one. See what God has done.

A grateful heart is a great start when it comes to tackling the difficulties of married life. And those difficulties come right at the get-go. At wedding receptions, I look for a time to be alone for a second or two with the bride and groom to say something like this: "Don't be disappointed if your first night together isn't easy. Sex is difficult. It takes practice. With time and practice, it will get better, so be patient and tender with each other tonight."

As with sexual intimacy, so with all the work of marriage: practice makes perfect. Each part of your life together is difficult to figure out how to do together, rather than alone.

Take canoeing, for instance. Yes, canoeing. Have you ever gone canoeing with your spouse? Picture a scenario with me, if you will...

Imagine the wife is an accomplished canoeist. She knows the J-stroke, for Pete's sake, and she could keep them headed in a straight line instead of veering from one shore to the other with no hope of finding the portage. She wonders if it would maybe possibly be okay to suggest—gently, of course—that she stern and he bow to her expertise? Yet there is that matter of her vow to obey, and might it not be unseemly to show her leadership in the matter of sternship? You say this is stupid, but it's these sorts of insecurities that fill up our decades of marriage.

Put yourself in the husband's mind and imagine he's ignorant of the first thing about canoeing. Yet, he doesn't want to encourage his wife to think poorly of him, so he tries to bluff his way through. He takes the stern and the canoe proceeds to veer from port to starboard, back to port, then back again to starboard. He does his best to keep things under control. He switches sides, throwing water off his paddle on his wife's back, and each switch threatens to capsize them.

Maybe they yell at each other. Maybe they burn quietly. Maybe they go home and brag to the other couples of their church what a good team they make in a canoe.

Such is marriage. Many of us run into something that silly, but that demoralizing, on our honeymoons (if not something much worse). Many of us don't make it a week into marriage without thinking, *This? This is it? This for the rest of my life?*

Yes, this, the rest of your life. And really, it's not so bad.

Not so bad? you respond.

Yup, not so bad. Stop and consider. You're no longer alone.

Some time ago, I was asked to preach at a marriage ceremony out north of Wichita, Kansas. The groom was the son of my former clerk of session up in Wisconsin. The son had gone off to Bible college and met the youngest daughter of a large Mennonite farm family, and they were to marry.

Kindly neighbors across the street from the bride's family allowed me to stay with them. There in a large basement room, furnished simply, with sun streaming in the windows high up the wall, I worked on my sermon. The text was

2 ISAAC WAS COMFORTED

Isaac and Rebekah's first meeting and wedding recorded in Genesis:

> Isaac went out to meditate in the field toward evening; and he lifted up his eyes and looked, and behold, camels were coming. Rebekah lifted up her eyes, and when she saw Isaac she dismounted from the camel. She said to the servant, "Who is that man walking in the field to meet us?" And the servant said, "He is my master." Then she took her veil and covered herself. The servant told Isaac all the things that he had done. (Gen. 24:63–66)

Why this account?

The whole record of God providing a wife for Abraham's son, Isaac, is about as beautiful as any love story could be. The work of Abraham's servant, who obviously loved his master. The scene at the well where the servant prayed, and in answer to his prayer, God caused Rebekah to offer to water his ten camels. (Likely she drew from the well and carried to each of the ten camels somewhere around thirty gallons apiece, so figure three hundred gallons at eight pounds per gallon for a total of 2,400 pounds she cheerfully carried that day—back and forth, back and forth.) That this hardworking woman was also "very beautiful, a virgin, and no man had had relations with her" (Gen. 24:16). Her feminine deference to Isaac when she was told this was the man who was to be her husband, dismounting her camel and veiling herself in modesty.

But my choice of text had little to do with any of these things. The very last verse of chapter 24 was what I was focused on:

> Then Isaac brought her into his mother Sarah's tent, and he

> took Rebekah, and she became his wife, and he loved her; thus Isaac was comforted after his mother's death.
>
> (Gen. 24:67)

Back home, I had been casting about for a text for the wedding. It's hard to decide on a text, and more so when those you are serving are some of the most loved of all the souls you have ever been privileged to work next to.[1] I wanted to serve him and his son and future daughter-in-law very well, so I was deep into the search for a text.

But then I had it. The bride was the last of eighteen children of this Mennonite farm family. Their kitchen and dining room were walls a few feet from an extremely long table custom made for a ton of people. It was the first thing I saw when I walked in the house. This daughter was godly and had nursed her mother through her dying days just a couple weeks earlier.

Now the father was experiencing the terrible fulfillment of his vow—"Till death separates us." His wife was gone. His family of forty or fifty was grieving. His daughter had just buried this mother she had served with such love, and now she was to marry. Of course it had to be this text.

The church was out in the farmland, all alone. Stark in its simplicity. Painted white with a wood floor, wood pews, and a platform. No banners. No colored paint. No stained glass windows. White, outside and inside. Full of humble souls, acutely aware of this joy of marriage and sorrow of the mother's death. The father had just said goodbye to his wife, and now he was saying goodbye to his precious youngest daughter.

Back in the early seventies, I'd never listened to country music, but I went to work for a guy who played bluegrass and turned me on to Merle Haggard. Haggard's song "Farmer's Daughter" is one of my favorites, and I've been listening to it as I write:

2 ISAAC WAS COMFORTED

Tonight there'll be candlelight and roses
In this little country chapel that's almost fallen down.
There'll be tears in this old farmer's eyes this evening
When I give my one possession to that city boy from town.

His hair is a little longer than we're used to,
But I guess I should find something good to say
About this man who's won the farmer's daughter
And will soon become my son-in-law today.

Mama left eight years ago December,
And it was hard to be a dad and mama too;
But somehow we made a home of this old farmhouse,
And love was all my baby ever knew.

He could be the richest man in seven counties
And not be good enough to take her hand,
But he says he really loves the farmer's daughter,
And I know the farmer's daughter loves the man.

Marriage is an event of new beginnings, but also of endings and separations and goodbyes. And it often can bring forgotten sadnesses to the surface. In my case, it was a few weeks after our honeymoon. Mary Lee and I were in worship Sunday morning, and the service ended with a hymn. Suddenly I couldn't stop crying. It was a new church plant where things were intimate, and I was embarrassed. What on earth?

We left quickly, but when we got home, I went to the bedroom and sobbed and sobbed. What on earth?

Mary Lee came in and sat on the bed trying to comfort me, and I sobbed even more. What on earth?

It took a while, but then it came over me in a wave.

Over a decade earlier on a cold January afternoon in Philadelphia, a small bedraggled clump of family and friends stood next to the grave of my nineteen-year-old brother, Joe. He'd had a sledding accident Christmas night. He was godly and sort of a father to me in the constant absence of Dad who was off preaching and speaking and putting together InterVarsity's *HIS Magazine* in Chicago two weeks each month.

The funeral had been held at Blue Church an hour earlier, but only a few people came to the graveside service. We stood there in the cold, praying and singing. Then we climbed in our car and drove out to the Midwest where Dad had taken a new job.

That graveside service was the end of all things Philadelphia for us. All our dear friends and their children were now over for us. Blue Church was over for us. Delaware County Christian School was over for us. Havertown was over for us. Swarthmore was over for Joe. Finishing our brief service there in Glenwood Memorial Gardens just off Westchester Pike, we climbed in our station wagon and drove away from it all—still mourning.

After we arrived in Bartlett, Illinois, things weren't easy. Joe was the third child my parents had lost to sickness and death. He was Dad's oldest son. Dad had had a new house built for us out in the country, in the middle of farmland. We were isolated, and Mud and Dad weren't getting along. In the days after Joe died, I'd been sent off to spend time with one of my teachers so Mud and Dad would have some relief from caring for their children as they grieved.

Really, though, as the days, months, and years passed, there was no space for Timmy to grieve. Mud and Dad's grief

2 ISAAC WAS COMFORTED

was raw, and anyone paying attention needed to help them, not their children.

Ten years later, God had just given me the most precious gift of my childhood sweetheart as my bride. And I loved her. Our honeymoon had been up on Lake Wisconsin during a terribly romantic ice storm, after which we moved to Madison. Then, there in church Sunday morning a few weeks later, our worship ended with this hymn:

> Savior, like a shepherd lead us,
> Much we need Thy tender care;
> In Thy pleasant pastures feed us,
> For our use Thy folds prepare:
> Blessed Jesus, blessed Jesus,
> Thou hast bought us, Thine we are;
> Blessed Jesus, blessed Jesus,
> Thou hast bought us, Thine we are.
>
> We are Thine; do Thou befriend us,
> Be the guardian of our way;
> Keep Thy flock, from sin defend us,
> Seek us when we go astray:
> Blessed Jesus, blessed Jesus,
> Hear, O hear us when we pray;
> Blessed Jesus, blessed Jesus,
> Hear, O hear us when we pray.
>
> Thou hast promised to receive us,
> Poor and sinful though we be;
> Thou hast mercy to relieve us,
> Grace to cleanse, and pow'r to free:
> Blessed Jesus, blessed Jesus,
> Let us early turn to Thee;

> Blessed Jesus, blessed Jesus,
> Let us early turn to Thee.
>
> Early let us seek Thy favor,
> Early let us do Thy will;
> Blessed Lord and only Savior,
> With Thy love our bosoms fill:
> Blessed Jesus, blessed Jesus,
> Thou hast loved us, love us still;
> Blessed Jesus, blessed Jesus,
> Thou hast loved us, love us still.[2]

I spent much of that Sunday afternoon grieving. I'm sure Mary Lee was distraught over my weakness and pain. For some time I had no idea what was wrong, but then it hit me. This was the hymn we sang at Joe's grave just before climbing in our car and driving off from where we'd buried him and from all the friends and loved ones I'd ever known.

But surely I'd sung this hymn many times since that day, so why the breakdown?

It came over me like a flood. Next to me was my wife. Finally I was safe and could grieve. She loved me and understood. She was my helpmate, so she caressed and comforted me. There, ten years later, I was comforted in the death of my brother Joe.

It was safe. It had not been good for me to be alone, and now I wasn't: I had my helpmate. Just as the man who married the young Mennonite woman had his. And just as you have yours.

God has given you the precious gift of a husband or wife to comfort you in this life's sorrows. What a precious gift. Fall into their arms. Sob. Grieve. Love.

Chapter 3
Male and Female

But from the beginning of creation,
God made them male and female.

— Mark 10:6

A couple years ago, Mary Lee and I were in New York City for a few days and visited the Metropolitan Museum of Art. We'd grown up outside Chicago, so we'd visited the Art Institute of Chicago a number of times, but those visits had always been more leisurely than this afternoon at the Met. We had Broadway tickets that evening so we had to move quickly. Floor after floor and gallery after gallery, we didn't stop and sit on any benches for deep communion with the artists and their work. In one way, this was helpful.

Blitzing through and getting quick impressions, we came to this conclusion: the Met's paintings of people generally fit into one of three categories: sin, pastoral scenes, and family life. A typical painting of the theme of sin was Rubens's *Lot and His Daughters*. A typical pastoral painting was Bruegel's *Harvesters*. And typical of the domestic scenes were the paintings of the Dutch master Jan Steen, championing the glorious unruliness of large family life.[1] Painting after painting, tender scenes with fathers, mothers, sons, and daughters, plus grandfathers, grandmothers, and the occasional neighbor and dog.

The old paintings had no celebration of androgyny. There weren't sexless "persons." There were men looking like men doing manly things and women looking beautiful doing feminine things. Daughters working alongside their mother and sons working alongside their father. Sex was everywhere on perfect display as God made us—male and female.

We also walked through Central Park that day, and the life of man[2] was on full display. Lovers walked every path and cuddled together on every wall, bench, and rock. They were overwhelmingly man and woman. Out in the real world that day, no one was fooling anyone. True life as God made it was out of the closet, and gays and lesbians were the abnormal ones. It was the center of Manhattan, but man loved woman and woman loved man.

After our flash tour of the Met, Mary Lee and I ran full tilt through pouring rain down to Broadway and had dinner, then went a couple doors over to take in *Hamilton*. Again, man and woman. In love. Sure, there was the decadent and hilariously effeminate King George, but he got all the laughs because he was decadent and effeminate. This was very much the point. But then there was Hamilton's love, but then also his betrayal of his wife—followed by his confession and her suffering, followed by her forgiveness. At that point I doubt there were many dry eyes. Certainly not my lover's and mine.

Why all this about paintings, parks, and plays?

"It is He who has made us, and not we ourselves" (Ps. 100:3). And who did He make us? "From the beginning, He made us male and female" (Matt. 19:4). Male and female are never "roles." Male and female are who God made us.

These days, the barrage of voices attacking God's beautiful creation of sexuality—the love of a man for a woman and their marriage and the fruitfulness of their marriage bed—assaults us until we almost think the world has flipped and become gay, bi, and trans. Then we look at paintings, walk in the park, and even take in a play on Broadway, and the romance of marriage between man and woman overwhelms all the perversions.

In his classic history of the decline and fall of the Roman Empire, Edward Gibbon notes the sexual decadence surrounding the New Testament church. Of the first fourteen emperors of Rome, only one was exclusively heterosexual.[3] The first Christians were distinctive in repenting of these sexual perversions all around them. Effeminates repented of their effeminacy, and men who had sex with other men did so no more.[4] Then, as the centuries passed, through the church's witness and practice, the beauty and love of man for woman increased and all the perversions were marginalized so that, in time, fidelity in male-and-female marriage prevailed. This is a large part of what we refer to as "Christendom," which spread through the Western world, prevailing for the next fifteen centuries—right up to our own time.

Now, though, Western culture's elite are intent upon legislating the reversal of Christendom's laws, spreading sexual degradation, particularly among the underclass.[5] We know the witness of the Early Church in such a climate, but what will be our witness?

Well, restoring the glory of male and female has a lot going for it. Even *Hamilton* and New York City couldn't help but testify to this. In our consciences, we all know it really does matter whom you love, because God made male and female and condemns all sexual intimacy outside heterosexual marriage.

But here's the thing, and readers must note this carefully: heterosexual marriage is far more than a man marrying a woman or a woman marrying a man. God wrote sexuality into so much more than the fit of body parts. "From the beginning He made them male and female" is not just about the beginning of time and the creation of Eve from and for Adam. Male and female is the distinction God puts in each of *us* at the very moment we are created by God.

From the moment of conception, every man and woman is one of two sexes. This sex He makes each of us is a command, not just about whom we are to marry and how we are to have intercourse, but about how we are to live. God made each of us a sexual being that is either male or female, and thus the male of our species is to obey his God-given maleness, and the female her God-given femaleness. Every moment of our lives.

Speaking of marriage specifically: As husband, the man is to look for ways to live out his manhood. As wife, the woman is to look for ways to live out her womanhood. Since God's diversity in creating male and female is a blessing to us, we are to look for ways to protect and honor that diversity. After all, God created it.

It may be helpful to think of the old saying, "Don't cut against the grain." A woodworker goes with the grain. He doesn't cut against it. And that's how we should live out our sexuality. Do what we were made to do. If a couple has to carry a heavy cooler to the beach and they have a nursing infant, the man, being stronger, carries the cooler, and the nursing mother carries the infant. Pretty basic, isn't it?

Multiply that principle across all of life and marriage, and sex becomes an asset—never a liability. Sure, the mother could carry the cooler and the father the nursing infant, if they preferred, but soon the baby would be hungry and the father would have to give the baby to the mother and take over carrying the cooler himself. At first the mother might prefer to carry the cooler to show how strong and independent she is. The father might prefer to carry the baby to show how sensitive and involved he is. But in time the mother would be nursing because she has been blessed with breasts, and the father would be carrying the cooler because he has upper body strength.

Are we too decadent to see this and rejoice in it? Why not simply thank God and luxuriate in the differences He has decreed for man and woman? Why not go with the grain?

When Mary Lee and I were first married, we were egalitarian feminists who promised each other we'd be different from our parents. Nothing would be determined by our sex. We would work, not according to our differences, but our preferences. The woman wouldn't necessarily cook, and the man wouldn't automatically change the car's oil. The woman wouldn't do anything just because she was a woman, nor the man just because he was a man. We'd negotiate things, and even our negotiations would be egalitarian. Which is to say, a stalemate.

It's no surprise that we fought all the time. I was taller and she was shorter, so when we walked, she went the speed she preferred, and I went the speed I preferred. Of course, we never talked about it. But during our walks, often there was a power play going on. An underlying tension.

Think of all the things normal couples decide by going with the grain of their sex. But with the two of us, every last one of these things could at any moment turn into a fight. Walking. Checking the oil on the car. Driving. Cooking. Cleaning up the kitchen. Doing the laundry. Balancing the checkbook. The power struggles were regular, and both of us were quite stubborn.

Then one day a Christian brother ten years older quietly said to me as we were taking a walk, "Tim, God wants you to lead your home." That one short sentence was all he uttered on the subject, but this brotherly rebuke started me thinking about authority in marriage; and once the door was opened, I began to think about authority everywhere.

It didn't take long for me to realize that I was a rebel and hated authority. Then it dawned on me that I couldn't lead my wife if I refused to submit to the authorities God had placed over *me* outside the home. I needed to repent and honor the law. Honor the civil authorities. Honor church authorities. Honor my professors. Pay my parking tickets.

The realizations kept going deeper and deeper. I was a rebel against authority, but the Christian obeys and honors authority. By God's grace, I had some considerable respect for my father and mother, so it wasn't as bad as it might have been. But almost everywhere else, there was hard work ahead.

Why are we talking about authority?

This is where sex began. God created Eve for Adam—not Adam for Eve. God created Eve to be Adam's helper—not Adam to be Eve's helper. God created Adam first, then Eve; and the significance of this for the authority of the man over the woman is opened up by the Apostle Paul when he commands,

> I do not allow a woman to teach or exercise authority over a man, but to remain quiet. For it was Adam who was first created, and then Eve. And it was not Adam who was deceived, but the woman being deceived, fell into transgression. But women will be preserved through the bearing of children if they continue in faith and love and sanctity with self-restraint.
> (1 Tim. 2:12–15)

Of course, the world and much of the Christian church today thinks of this passage as toxic masculinity at its worst.

3 MALE AND FEMALE

Adam was created "first" and "then Eve"? So Adam is the first and Eve the second sex, right? Isn't that precisely what Simone de Beauvoir attacked in her book *The Second Sex*?

Beauvoir's work was published in 1949, and it stoked a smoldering fire that now has grown into a worldwide conflagration, not just among unbelievers, but sadly (because we should know better) also within the Christian church and home. There's not a marriage or family, not a husband or wife, not a father or mother, not a son or daughter, not a congregation or pulpit this wildfire has not singed and charred.

Precisely what is it Beauvoir despised and attacked?

> In Genesis . . . Eve is depicted as made from . . . Adam.
>
> Thus humanity is male and man defines woman not in herself but as relative to him . . .
>
> Legislators, priests, philosophers, writers, and scientists have striven to show that the subordinate position of woman is willed in heaven and advantageous on earth. The religions invented by men reflect this wish for domination. In the legends of Eve and Pandora men have taken up arms against women.[6]

You got that, right? "The religions invented by men." She's speaking of our most holy faith revealed by God in His Word.

Leaving Beauvoir behind, let's tune our minds and hearts to God and His Word. There we read that, from the beginning—prior to the Fall—God made woman to be Adam's helper, the helper that by God's design is "meet," or suitable, for him.

What is a helper?

A helper doesn't lead. She follows. This is her gift to the leader. This is the helper's orientation. The caboose doesn't claw his way up the train to get ahead of the locomotive.

Woman can't honor God's creation order and the sex God made her, then spend her life resenting that woman is man's helper.

Here is the beginning of wisdom concerning marriage. Man was not created for woman, but woman for man. See how detailed God's Word is concerning this creation order of Adam and Eve:

> [Man] is the image and glory of God; but the woman is the glory of man. For man does not originate from woman, but woman from man; for indeed man was not created for the woman's sake, but woman for the man's sake. (1 Cor. 11:7–9)

If the Holy Spirit had been concerned that the church might grow confused about this in the late twentieth and early twenty-first centuries, how would we suggest He speak with greater clarity than He's spoken through the Apostle Paul here in 1 Corinthians 11?

It's easy to imagine someone reading this and reacting in anger: *Why put it so negatively? The point isn't the order of the sexes, but the beauty of two persons loving each other and not having to go through life alone.*

But there we have it: the Holy Spirit inspired the Apostle Paul to be very firm and clear on just that—the order of the sexes established by God at Creation, prior to the Fall while all things were still perfect.

I mention when this happened because there are many false shepherds seeking to harm your soul by preaching and teaching that the authority of man in relation to woman is not as God intended it. They spread the false doctrine that the husband's headship is only a result of our sinfulness, which of course means it was the decay brought into the life of man *after* the Fall.

Clearly not. God created Adam first, then Eve. In the garden of Eden. Before the Fall.

The authority of Adam was no design flaw or failure. It was God's perfect design feature, and thus His blessing. But not just for Adam. Also for Eve. His blessing not just for man. Also for woman. Contrary to what the whole world is screaming today outside and inside the church, authority and submission are not a curse. We received both from God back in the state of perfection, and thus they are our blessings.

Scripture records that God Himself has delegated His authority to those who are over us. And the Word of God never apologizes that these authorities are always and everywhere sinners. Nor does God apologize that the men and women He commands to submit are sinners.

> Every person is to be in subjection to the governing authorities. For there is no authority except from God, and those which exist are established by God. Therefore whoever resists authority has opposed the ordinance of God; and they who have opposed will receive condemnation upon themselves. (Rom. 13:1–2)

Every human society and organization is ordered by God. The family is the basic unit of society, and marriage is the basic unit of the family. God has decreed the husband to be the head of his wife, and the father the head of the household. We may beat our fists against it all we want, but it will only result in our receiving God's "condemnation" upon ourselves, because He is the origin of all authority. Even the henhouse has its pecking order, testifying to us the universal rule of authority God has written across all Creation. Adam named the animals. Adam also named Eve. Naming is authority, and this authority was given Adam by God.

Here are two places Scripture testifies to this order, which I discovered only a few years ago.

First, notice Moses' record of the words of God to Noah concerning the animals he was to take into his ark:

> You shall take with you of every clean animal by sevens, a male and his female; and of the animals that are not clean two, a male and his female. (Gen. 7:2)[7]

The possessive pronoun "his" is the way English expresses the Hebrew text indicating the relationship of the female to the male. This is not something Moses himself wrote because he was a chauvinist who lived in an ancient patriarchal culture. Moses was simply documenting God's words to Noah. "A male and his female." In Hebrew, the words are *ish* and *ishshah*, which are the same words used by Adam when he explains, "She shall be called Woman [*ishshah*], because she was taken out of Man [*ish*]" (Gen. 2:23). A man and *his* woman.

Second, notice how the Apostle Paul describes the relationship of the lesbians of the Roman Empire to the men of that Empire:

> God gave them over to degrading passions; for their women exchanged the natural function for that which is unnatural. (Rom. 1:26)

Again, note the possessive pronoun "their."[8] Small words communicate large truths, and again, the truth communicated by "their" is that the first woman, Eve, was created for and from the first man, Adam. Man is the glory of God, and woman the glory of man.

What is the meaning and significance of all this biblical

witness to the creation order of Adam first, then Eve? Scripture teaches us the practical implications for wives:

> You wives, be submissive to your own husbands so that even if any of them are disobedient to the word, they may be won without a word by the behavior of their wives. (1 Pet. 3:1)

And:

> Wives, be subject to your own husbands, as to the Lord. For the husband is the head of the wife, as Christ also is the head of the church, He Himself being the Savior of the body. But as the church is subject to Christ, so also the wives ought to be to their husbands in everything. (Eph. 5:22–24)

The wife is to be subject to her own husband. Not to every man, but to her own husband. And subject to him in everything.

What of husbands?

Scripture says:

> Husbands, love your wives, just as Christ also loved the church and gave Himself up for her, so that He might sanctify her, having cleansed her by the washing of water with the word, that He might present to Himself the church in all her glory, having no spot or wrinkle or any such thing; but that she would be holy and blameless. So husbands ought also to love their own wives as their own bodies. He who loves his own wife loves himself. (Eph. 5:25–28)

The husband is to love his wife. Not every woman, but his own wife. The husband is to give himself up for his wife. The husband is to sanctify his wife. To cleanse his wife by the washing of water with the Word. He is to love his own wife as his own body. To love his wife as he loves himself. Think of our Lord's love for the church. His love isn't some sentimental gushing, but constant hard work and instruction followed by death. He does good to us and cares for our welfare. His love is more actions than feelings, so we might say, "He who does good for his own wife does good for himself."

Scripture also has a warning for husbands:

> Love your wives and do not be embittered against them.
> (Col. 3:19)

Marriage is hard. The husband is to love his wife, yes. But he's also commanded *not* to become embittered against her.

Scripture also says:

> You husbands in the same way, live with your wives in an understanding way, as with someone weaker, since she is a woman; and show her honor as a fellow heir of the grace of life, so that your prayers will not be hindered. (1 Pet. 3:7)

The husband is to live with his wife in an understanding way, knowing that, since she is a woman and not a man, she is weaker. The husband is to show honor to his wife since she is a fellow heir of the grace of life. Otherwise his prayers will be hindered.

We could continue, but isn't the point clear? If we were to examine carefully all Scripture's commands concerning the duties of husbands and wives to one another, an accurate summary would be that wives are to submit to their husbands and husbands are to love their wives. The woman is to be her husband's fitting helper and the husband is to love her tenderly—as tenderly and sacrificially as Christ loves His Bride, the Church.

Our problem is not lack of clarity or difficulty of application, but once again (as with the fruitfulness of the marriage bed), our problem is that we lack faith. To paraphrase an old curmudgeon, the problem is not that submitting to our husband has been tried and found difficult, but that it has been found difficult and left untried. The problem is not that loving our wife has been tried and found difficult, but that it has been found difficult and left untried. In other words, it's not the concepts of submission and love we have trouble with, but the doing of them.

But God made us, so He knows we need things repeated. He knows how weak we are—that we are made of dust. So, He fills His Scripture with these commands. We must have them repeated again and again so we won't give in to the false shepherds breeding rebellion through their twisting of God's words. We also need them repeated so we won't give in to our flesh and pride, living the very opposite of the submission and love we are commanded to give to our husband and wife.

Yes, there are times to disobey a wicked husband, but their existence doesn't justify rebelling the vast majority of times when what we're told by God is to submit. To obey.

Sometimes in counseling couples about what submission looks like in marriage, I suggest the wife check her own heart and will by noting her husband's preferences and seeing if she's willing to serve them. Not in big things like where he wants the children to be schooled, but little things like what the family has for dinner. The wife who is cheerfully submissive will not obstruct her husband's known preferences for this or that vegetable or bread. She'll take joy in giving it to him. Little things like choice of menu, favorite chair, and toothpaste caps say a lot.

And note I'm not speaking to the husband, but the wife. My examples for how a husband tells if he's loving his wife vary by couple, but I often notice two equal and opposite errors.

Some husbands are "little men," insecure and selfish, constantly making rules about the stupidest things and then barking at their wives and children if they don't obey. This is the most certain way of undermining your authority in the home, and it's one of the central failures that cause children to become exasperated with you, contrary to what Scripture commands: "Fathers, do not exasperate your children, so that they will not lose heart" (Col. 3:21).

But husbands who are not controlling often fail to love their wives when they refuse to take responsibility and make decisions. Where should they go to dinner? How much should they give to their church's capital campaign? Where should they go to church? Whose in-laws should they visit for Thanksgiving this year? What rude behavior of which child at the dinner table should be overlooked, what rebuked, and what disciplined? When should it be responded to, and if discipline is in order, who should do it, and how?

Often, husbands want to avoid conflict, so they avoid making these decisions, or even expressing an opinion about them. Some husbands try to sell their abdication as servant leadership, as in, "Honey, what do you think we should do?" In many cases, such a response is merely a cover for laziness. The husband hates conflict and does anything he can to avoid being the bad guy. When his wife complains about his passivity, such a husband might become slightly aggressive and respond, "Look, at work I spend all day dealing with conflict and I'm sick of it. Can't I have a little peace and quiet at home? Handle it."

Such a man is not loving his wife or giving himself up for

her. He's loving only himself. Taking responsibility isn't easy, but it's what husbands and fathers are called by God to do, and doing so is one of the kindest, sweetest, most loving gifts we can ever give our wives.

To sum up this chapter, the husband and wife are not simply two persons, but one man and one woman. We are to live in obedience to our sex, not just because God assigned it to us, but because it will be working with the grain of our marriage and family life. Our faithfulness to our manhood and womanhood will create a safe space for our sons and daughters to grow into their own manhood and womanhood. They'll have models to watch, yes—but also, they'll feel safe.

And that's the best part, isn't it? That our sons and daughters grow into godliness, and toward raising children of their own who will honor God—not just as persons, but as the men and women God made them.

May God give you faith to obey and love the nature and duties of your manhood or womanhood. Many of us before you have walked this difficult path, often while professors, teachers, pastors, and even our own parents have tried to lead us into rebellion.

Don't listen. It is the Lord's approval we are seeking.

Chapter 4
The Best Wedding Gift

> When a man takes a new wife, he shall not go out with the army nor be charged with any duty; he shall be free at home one year and shall give happiness to his wife whom he has taken.
>
> — Deuteronomy 24:5

In the law that heads this chapter, the tenderness of God towards a new bride is on full display. From His concern for her, He forbids her husband to go off to war for at least one year following marriage. Instead the husband is to spend that year giving "happiness to his wife."

Think about that. Husband, did you spend your first year of marriage giving happiness to your bride?

Likely many of us are embarrassed by this question and have deep regrets.

Mary Lee and I have done a lot of premarital counseling, and one of the warnings we give engaged couples is that the man's focus will change after the wedding ceremony and honeymoon. Right now, his task is to close the deal, as it were, but this is almost certain to change. After the wedding he'll still be task oriented, but his focus will have changed.

By the way, José Ortega y Gasset once pointed out that all true thinking begins with exaggeration.[1] Please bear with my generalizations about men and women. Yes, there are exceptions, but generalizations will be essential for you and your spouse. Yes, not every man has larger shoulders than every woman, nor does every woman have larger hips than every man. There are exceptions to this rule, but speaking generally, men have larger shoulders and women have larger hips. So let's all take a deep breath and allow ourselves to think about this matter of the groom's task orientation.

Before marriage, the man is focused on getting his bride and tying the knot, so he's spending lots of time listening to her talk about flowers and dresses and this and that friend who should or shouldn't be asked to be a bridesmaid. They stay up late at night talking and talking, but keep in mind the man is not married yet. The goal is right in front of him and he's pursuing it with emotional intelligence and sensitivity, so at this stage in their relationship he's not likely to run from communication and intimacy.

Once married, though, he is tempted to think these tasks are accomplished. She is his bride, so new goals are in front of them and those goals require a different set of skills. He must provide for his new household. He must get a better job. He must figure out how to finish his education. He must assure his male friends he's still the same man he was before he was married.

Meanwhile, his bride has not lost any of her desire for emotional intimacy with her bridegroom. Before the wedding, he was her lover. Before the wedding, he talked to her for hours. Before the wedding, he responded immediately to her phone calls and texts. Before the wedding, he was sensitive, gentle, and communicative. Before the wedding, he was focused on making his lover happy.

Now though, not so much. After all, he made her happy, didn't he? Aren't they married? It was a big job, but it's done.

The knot is tied and now he's moved on to his next task. After her honeymoon, the bride often feels as if her personhood and emotional needs have been relegated, and likely she's right.

But trust me when I point out that the groom is going to be relegated as well (emotionally and in other ways). But that doesn't happen until the baby in the baby carriage. Mothers awaiting the birth of their first child are one person before the child is born and a completely different person the moment that newborn is placed at her breast. She has become Mother. She will not stop being Mother until the moment of her death, and Mother is not lover, bride, or wife. Or maybe it's better to say, Mother trumps lover, bride, and wife.

After the birth of a first child, I often ask the new dad whether he has felt any jealousy towards his newborn. If we dig deep enough (sometimes we don't have to dig much at all), usually the answer is yes.

So now, back to this Old Testament law that new husbands not go off to war during their first year of marriage. Many men have left for boot camp or been deployed within days of their wedding. You've read about them and know the anguish of their letters to their new bride. We also are aware of the pain of the new bride as she says goodbye to her husband who might not return. That's war, after all.[2] But in the normal course of things, God calls a husband to spend his first year of marriage giving "happiness to the wife he has taken."

As I said before, this part of the law is based on a principle. And this principle doesn't just apply to deployment, but also to grad school, seminary, and work. It applies to turning away from your own family relationships and turning towards your wife in order to establish your own relationships in your new home. The principle applies to those male friendships that demand you go out hunting, drinking, playing softball, playing board games, seeing movies—acting as if you're still single.

Husband, you are no longer the man you were before taking your vows. God has given you your wife, and your first year of marriage you would do well to focus on making her happy.

This wisdom should be part of the church's teaching and pastoral care among God's people. Pastors, elders, and older women of the church should talk about it and help couples understand how helpful this principle is. We should suggest ways to take it into account and act on it. And we should remember that the principle is not simply that husbands should not go to war during the first year of marriage, but that husbands should spend their first year of marriage giving happiness to their wife. It's *because* of this principle that a husband should not go to war during that year. Doing so will make his wife sad.

But how exactly are you supposed to make your wife *happy*?

First of all, understand that making your wife happy doesn't mean agreeing with her every opinion and fulfilling her every desire. Not in the first year, not in the last year, and not during all those years in between. There will be plenty of times to say yes to your wife, and plenty of times to say no. But do you want to know what will really make her happy? Saying no to yourself.

Take, for instance, the husband who tells his wife that he's feeling called into pastoral ministry. She agrees he has the gifting, and their church affirms it too. So should they go straight from the wedding and move across the country to start seminary?

Maybe not. Instead, this husband might decide to make

his wife happy by putting off seminary for a year or two so he and his bride will have time together at home kissing and talking and reading and taking walks. This is quite different from seminary life when the husband is off at the library and in classes and up late at night writing papers, rather than being in bed next to his sweetheart.

Rita Cuffey was a dear sister in Christ whom I met with weekly here in Bloomington for over a decade. She was in her late eighties when she told me she met her husband Jimmy at Harvard when they were both grad students in astronomy. When Jimmy asked her to marry him, she went to see her supervising professor to tell him she wouldn't be needing her funded research position anymore.

She was brilliant and disciplined, so of course the professor didn't want to lose her. He responded, "Rita, you don't need to resign your fellowship just because you're getting married. Stay in the program as a married woman and we'll keep the money coming."

Short little Italian Rita Paraboschi, born and raised in Boston's North End, responded, "But I don't want to continue. I'd much rather be home in bed warm next to Jimmy than out at the observatory looking at the sky and cold." Rita was one of the godliest women I've known, and despite the cost to their finances and her ego (if she had one), what made Rita happy was giving up her doctoral studies for the warmth of her marriage bed.

Should a husband do any less for his wife? What shift do you work? How far do you drive to work each day? Do you play iPhone games at night rather than talking to your wife?

When a husband's job asks him to move across the country for another position right after their marriage, he might well decline, explaining that he wants to stay put for a year or two so he and his wife can get their home off to a good start.

4 THE BEST WEDDING GIFT

When the local Christian high school asks him to coach basketball or soccer, he might ask the school to keep him in mind for future seasons. If they both work but have low-paying jobs, and the husband's parents live nearby, have extra space in their home, and don't need any rent, the husband would do well to say no to their kind housing offer, knowing that living in their home the first year of marriage would not be his wife's happy place.

One final word about your wife's happiness.

Let me warn you that one of the most common mistakes Christian husbands and wives make in their first year of marriage is using some form of contraception to put off having children. I've heard all the reasons: Student loans need to be paid off. The couple wants to take a year to really concentrate on getting to know each other. The husband isn't ready for the responsibility of fatherhood. The wife isn't ready for the ceaseless demands of motherhood. The wife's parents made her promise that after the wedding ceremony she would not get pregnant until she had finished college and was established in her career. Life is long and there's plenty of time later in life. We already have a dog and cat. We want to travel. Our apartment is too small...

Listen. If we're really concerned to make our wives happy, we need to cherish the life-givingness of her feminine body and soul, recognizing how central the bearing of children is to her happiness.[3] This is evidenced by the visceral pain common among couples who suffer infertility. It's a dreadful ache that will not go away.

Some of us had children our first year of marriage. God blessed us with a fruitful womb so that we had the great joy of welcoming children into our home and marriage early. First came love, then came marriage, then came our baby in a baby carriage. What joy for the new father. What contentment for the new mother. What happiness for the new wife.

If you want to make your wife happy, love and encourage her fruitfulness. Let her know there's nothing that gives you more pleasure than seeing God bless your marriage and home with the fruit of your love. Tell her your joy would be full if she presented you with a little boy or girl that looks and acts and talks like her.

Let's be honest. If you wait too long, your wife might decide she loves the perks of a career and vacations and eating out and building a new house and cooing over her cat sitting in her lap, and you will run the risk of relegating motherhood, fatherhood, and children in her heart. Where her treasure is, there her heart will be also, so treasure her motherhood.

Priorities are set early in marriage, and children have a way of firming up what our unity and commitments are as husband and wife. If you choose to put off children, you may discover it was a terribly expensive mistake that you will regret the rest of your life.

But you will never regret receiving the blessing of a little one from the hand of God. Receiving a child from God as the fruit of your love will build that love and commitment that is perfectly designed to make every woman happy.

And don't you want to make your wife happy?

Chapter 5

What about Birth Control?

Behold, children are a gift of the LORD,
The fruit of the womb is a reward.

— Psalm 127:3

In 1930, the Anglicans became the first Christian denomination to endorse the use of contraception. At their decennial Lambeth Conference, three hundred bishops passed a resolution declaring Christian husbands and wives were free to obstruct the union of sperm and egg in order to "limit or avoid parenthood."[1]

Never before had the Church said such a thing.

And it wasn't because various forms of contraception and birth control had not existed before 1930. Go all the way back to Genesis. Onan used withdrawal to avoid having a child with his deceased brother's wife (contrary to his father's command). He was condemned by God, and spilling

---

1. ". . . in those cases where there is such a clearly felt moral obligation to limit or avoid parenthood, and where there is a morally sound reason for avoiding complete abstinence, the Conference agrees that other methods may be used . . ." Resolution 15 from The Lambeth Conference, 1930, Anglican Communion, accessed December 3, 2021, https://www.anglicancommunion.org/resources/document-library/lambeth-conference/1930/resolution-15-the-life-and-witness-of-the-christian-community-marriage.aspx.

seed during intercourse came to be called "Onanism."[2] Across Christian history, Eastern Orthodox, Roman Catholic, and Protestant Christians have always taught that the account of God's punishment of Onan was not simply the condemnation of Onan for refusing to give his brother's wife a child, but more foundationally, God's condemnation of contraceptive methods used to render lovemaking sterile—to "limit or avoid parenthood," as the Anglicans put it. The Church has always stood against contraception and birth control.

Now, if you're the sort of person who thinks our modern era finally got it right (after thousands of years of Christians being stupid on the subject), I can only say you have a lot to learn about respect for authority and the wisdom of our

---

2. See Genesis 38:6–10.

3. See chapter 2 of the *Didache*. Some English translations render the Greek *pharmakeia* as "sorcery" rather than "birth control." In his classic work on contraception, John T. Noonan Jr. explains that "*Pharmakeia* . . . is the employment of drugs with occult properties for a variety of purposes, including, in particular, contraception or abortion." "Abortion and the Catholic Church: A Summary History," *Natural Law Forum* 12 (1967): 90–91, accessed December 3, 2021, https://scholarship.law.nd.edu/nd_naturallaw_forum/126.

4. "Women who resort to some sort of deadly abortion drug kill not only the embryo, but along with it, all human kindness." Clement of Alexandria, *Paedagogus* 2.10.96, as translated by Simon P. Wood in *Christ the Educator*, vol. 23 of The Fathers of the Church (Catholic University of America Press, 1954), 173–174.

5. "In our case, murder being once for all forbidden, we may not destroy even the fetus in the womb, while as yet the human being derives blood from other parts of the body for its sustenance. To hinder a birth is merely a speedier man-killing; nor does it matter whether you take away a life that is born, or destroy one that is coming to the birth." Tertullian, *Apology* 9, in *Ante-Nicene Fathers*, vol. 3.

6. ". . . women, reputed believers, began to resort to drugs for producing sterility, and to gird themselves round, so to expel what was being conceived on account of their not wishing to have a child . . ." Hippolytus, *Refutation of All Heresies* 9.7, in *Ante-Nicene Fathers*, vol. 5.

7. "Why do you sow where the field is eager to destroy the fruit? Where there are medicines of sterility? Where there is murder before the birth? You do not even let a harlot remain only a harlot, but you make her a murderess

5 WHAT ABOUT BIRTH CONTROL?

elders. In any case, let me reiterate: the Church has always been united on this subject.

Need proof? Start with the second-century catechism used to instruct believers in the basics of Christian faith and practice called *The Teaching of the Twelve Apostles*—or, more commonly, the *Didache*: "You shall not practice birth control, you shall not murder a child by abortion, nor kill what is begotten."[3]

Then read the works of Early Church fathers such as Clement of Alexandria,[4] Tertullian,[5] Hippolytus,[6] John Chrysostom,[7] and Augustine.[8] You can get a medieval perspective from Thomas Aquinas.[9] And a Reformed one from Martin Luther[10] and John Calvin.[11] A Puritan one from Jeremy

---

as well. . . . Indeed, it is something worse than murder and I do not know what to call it; for she does not kill what is formed but prevents its formation. What then? Do you contemn the gift of God, and fight with his law? What is a curse, do you seek as though it were a blessing?" Chrysostom, Homily 24 on Romans, in John T. Noonan, *Contraception: A History of Its Treatment by Catholic Theologians and Canonists* (The Belknap Press of Harvard University, 1965), 98.

8. "Intercourse, even with one's lawfully wedded spouse, can take place in an unlawful and shameful manner, whenever the conception of offspring is avoided. Onan, the son of Judah, did this very thing, and the Lord slew him on that account." Augustine of Hippo, *Adulterous Marriages* 2.12, as translated in *Saint Augustine: Treatises on Marriage and Other Subjects*, vol. 27 of The Fathers of the Church (Catholic University of America Press, 1969), 117.

9. "The emission of semen apart from the proper purpose of generating and bringing up children . . . is incompatible with the natural good; namely, the preservation of the species. Hence, after the sin of homicide whereby a human nature already in existence is destroyed, this type of sin appears to take next place, for by it the generation of human nature is precluded. Moreover, these views which have just been given have a solid basis in divine authority. That the emission of semen under conditions in which offspring cannot follow is illicit is quite clear." Thomas Aquinas, *Summa Contra Gentiles* 3.2.122.9–10, trans. Vernon J. Bourke, accessed January 17, 2022, https://isidore.co/aquinas/english/ContraGentiles3b.htm#122.

10. "Onan must have been a malicious and incorrigible scoundrel. This is a most disgraceful sin. It is far more atrocious than incest and adultery. We call it unchastity, yes, a Sodomitic sin. For Onan goes in to her; that is, he

Taylor.[12] And let's not leave out the founder of Methodism, John Wesley.[13]

Go ahead and read the footnotes. I'll wait. My editors didn't want pages and pages of block quotes, but I didn't want to relegate everything to an appendix. Or worse, leave it out altogether. I wanted you to be able to see and read for yourself a small sampling of the mass of text from thousands of years of church history and practice. All of it vehemently, undeniably against birth control and contraception.

---

lies with her and copulates, and when it comes to the point of insemination, spills the semen, lest the woman conceive. Surely at such a time the order of nature established by God in procreation should be followed. Accordingly, it was a most disgraceful crime to produce semen and excite the woman, and to frustrate her at that very moment." Martin Luther, *Lectures on Genesis: Chapters 38–44*, Luther's Works, vol. 7, ed. Jaroslav Pelikan (Concordia Publishing House, 1965), 20–21.

11. "The voluntary spilling of semen outside of intercourse between man and woman is a monstrous thing. Deliberately to withdraw from coitus in order that semen may fall to the ground is doubly monstrous. For this is to extinguish the hope of the race and to kill before he is born—the hoped for offspring." John Calvin, comments on Genesis 38:10, trans. Ford Lewis Battles.

12. "'He is an ill husband, that uses his wife as a man treats a harlot, having no other end but pleasure.' Concerning which our best rule is, that although in this, as in eating and drinking, there is an appetite to be satisfied, which cannot be done without pleasing that desire; yet since that desire and satisfaction was intended by nature for other ends, they should never be separate from those ends, but always be joined with all or one of these ends, . . . but never with a purpose, either in act or desire, to separate the sensuality from these ends which hallow it. Onan did separate his act from its proper end, and so ordered his embraces that his wife should not conceive, and God punished him." "Rules for Married Persons, or Matrimonial Chastity," *Holy Living* (Christian Classics Ethereal Library), 106, accessed January 18, 2022, https://www.ccel.org/ccel/t/taylor/holy_living/cache/holy_living.pdf.

13. "Onan, though he consented to marry the widow, yet to the great abuse of his own body, of the wife he had married, and the memory of his brother that was gone, he refused to raise up seed unto his brother. Those sins that dishonour the body are very displeasing to God, and the evidence of vile actions. Observe, the thing which he did displeased the Lord—And it is to be feared, thousands, especially of single persons, by this very thing,

5 WHAT ABOUT BIRTH CONTROL?

Such opposition continued into the nineteenth[14] and twentieth centuries. German Lutheran pastor and theologian Dietrich Bonhoeffer was against it.[15] Even C. S. Lewis, who departed from Christian orthodoxy on several points, found little reason to stray from Christian teaching on this one.[16] And Pope Paul VI's *Humanae vitae* from 1968 reflects the long-standing opposition of Roman Catholics to contraception.[17]

As you read the footnotes, you probably noticed how

---

still displeased the Lord, and destroy their own souls." John Wesley, *Notes on the Bible*, Genesis 38:7ff.

14. In 1888 the Reformed Presbyterian Church declared: "We believe that uncleanness, in all its polluting and debasing forms, is increasing. We fear that many, who are members of the Church, employ means to prevent offspring, using the marriage bed to gratify their lusts, destroying their own lives, and bringing on themselves the wrath of a holy God." "Causes of Fasting and Thanksgiving" (item 8), from Minutes of the of the Reformed Presbyterian Church, 1888, accessed January 18, 2022, https://www.covenanter.org/reformed/2015/7/30/1888.

15. "The right of nascent life is violated also in the case of a marriage in which the emergence of new life is consistently prevented, a marriage in which the desire for a child is consistently excluded. Such an attitude is in contradiction to the meaning of marriage itself and to the blessing which God has bestowed upon marriage through the birth of the child." Dietrich Bonhoeffer, *Ethics*, trans. Neville Horton Smith (Macmillan, 1965), 176.

16. "As regards contraceptives, there is a paradoxical, negative sense in which all possible future generations are the patients or subjects of a power wielded by those already alive. By contraception simply, they are denied existence; by contraception used as a means of selective breeding, they are, without their concurring voice, made to be what one generation, for its own reasons, may choose to prefer. From this point of view, what we call Man's power over Nature turns out to be a power exercised by some men over other men with Nature as its instrument. . . . All long-term exercises of power, especially in breeding, must mean the power of earlier generations over later ones." C. S. Lewis, *The Abolition of Man* (HarperCollins, 1944), ch. 3.

17. "An act of mutual love which impairs the capacity to transmit life which God the Creator, through specific laws, has built into it, frustrates His design which constitutes the norm of marriage, and contradicts the will of the Author of life." *Humanae vitae* (*Of Human Life*) (sec. 13), July 25, 1968, accessed January 18, 2022, http://www.vatican.va/content/paul-vi/en/encyclicals/documents/hf_p-vi_enc_25071968_humanae-vitae.html.

those who came before us made little distinction between *contraception* (preventing the fertilization of the egg by the sperm) and *abortion* (destroying the baby created by the fertilization of the egg by the sperm). They do make a distinction between the two, but that distinction is cloudy to them. In some degree, this is due to their relative lack of knowledge regarding the scientific details of reproduction. Because of this, some readers might argue that it was merely the *possibility* of killing the unborn baby which the church through the ages has opposed. Such readers might go on to assert that we today have a better understanding of anatomy, as well as the agency of chemicals and other artificial means of preventing the conception of a new human being, and that our scientific understanding proves these means don't harm babies so that now we know it is fine to prevent children during lovemaking.

Such thinking has ushered in a cornucopia of methods, devices, and drugs which have become firmly established within the church. Sadly, though, our presumption is unwarranted. If we're willing to be humble, we'll notice a few things before we judge our fathers in the faith.

First, what our church fathers lacked in scientific understanding, they made up for in wisdom. The creation of new life is a great mystery. Every new piece of knowledge we gain from science merely reveals far more that we don't know. Our fathers had the wisdom and self-awareness to tread cautiously on matters of such mystery.

Second, the principal source for our fathers' condemnation of dividing the unitive and procreative functions of marital intercourse has always been God's condemnation of Onan in Genesis 38. But notice that Onan's method of contraception was unmistakably contraceptive—not abortive. His withdrawal kept the sperm from the egg, and thus all the

5 WHAT ABOUT BIRTH CONTROL?

church fathers who condemned Onan's sin knew they were not condemning murder, but the avoidance of conception altogether.

Third, the chemicals and artificial means now firmly established within the church under the justification that they prevent the union of sperm and egg (and that they do not kill the child conceived by that union) have always been known to work not only by preventing conception, but also by aborting (killing) the conceived child.[18]

Here's the problem. For decades now, scientists and the media (including the American College of Obstetricians and Gynecologists) have promoted the lie that conception doesn't occur until the attachment of the newly fertilized egg on the wall of his mother's uterus. And yet the egg has been fertilized by the sperm, creating one unique individual bearing

---

18. Even a cursory search online will demonstrate how tenuous it is to claim common contraceptive techniques are not abortive. For a brief, careful take on the subject, see Randy Alcorn, *Does the Birth Control Pill Cause Abortions?*, a summary of which can be found at https://www.epm.org/resources/2010/Feb/17/short-condensation-does-birth-control-pill-cause-a/.

The same conclusions can be found in secular sources: "There has been a gradual but major change in oral contraception. The drive to reduce metabolic assault and unwanted side-effects has resulted in a trend toward formulations which are less contraceptive and more likely to be abortifacient." Nicholas Tonti-Filippini, "The Pill: Abortifacient or Contraceptive?," *The Linacre Quarterly* 62, no. 1 (February 1995): 5, accessed January 18, 2022, https://doi.org/10.1080/20508549.1995.11878286. And one more: "[In] Most of the scientific community, . . . when referring to the unborn embryo, pregnancy must be defined as the period extending from implantation to natural birth. This implies some novelty, such as the redefinition of abortion as the elimination of the embryo only within this period, and the extension of contraception to any means that impedes the union of the gametes as a consequence of a sexual intercourse, or also that which eliminates the product of conception prior to its implantation. Therefore, the pharmaceutical industry markets, under the name of contraceptives, products that act also by means of an anti-implantation mechanism." Pau Agulles Simó, "Abortifacient effect of hormonal contraceptives: a review" (abstract), *Cuadernos de Bioética* 26, no. 86 (January–April 2015): 69, accessed January 18, 2022, https://pubmed.ncbi.nlm.nih.gov/26030015/.

the image of God. But science denies he exists if he hasn't yet attached himself to his mother's womb. This lie has allowed Christians to tell ourselves our pills don't kill our babies.

But we aren't thereby innocent of our bloodguilt. For decades it has been a fact known and easily confirmed (in pharmacists' continuing education literature distributed by pharmaceutical firms, for instance) that the Pill's agency is not simply the prevention of fertilization, but also the rendering of the uterine wall inhospitable to the new little one seeking to attach herself so she may receive sustenance from her mother.[19] This is also one part of the agency of what are sometimes known as "morning after" pills now available over the counter and widely used in the church. It is true *most* of their agency is to prevent fertilization, but they also work through *aborting* the little one when fertilization *does* occur.

Do Christians care that our use of such chemicals has left blood on our hands?

These words are not scare tactics. Read the literature.

Sadly, while we condemn Democrat politicians for promoting late-term abortions, we Christians have been practicing early-term abortions. Since the mainstreaming of abortive birth control methods (IUDs, Depo-Provera, the Pill, Plan B, etc.), the church has lost many of her children through mothers and fathers rendering the mother's womb inhospitable to their little one so that the little one is sloughed off and dies. John Calvin explains well why this killing in the womb should be abhorrent to us:

---

19. See, for instance, Grant D. E. McWilliams and John L. Fratarelli, "Changes in measured endometrial thickness predict in vitro fertilization success," *Fertility and Sterility* 88, no. 1 (July 2007): 74–81, https://doi.org/10.1016/j.fertnstert.2006.11.089; Stephen G. Somkuti et al., "The effect of oral contraceptive pills on markers of endometrial receptivity," *Fertility and Sterility* 65, no. 3 (March 1996): 484–488, https://doi.org/10.1016/S0015-0282(16)58141-2.

> If it seems more horrible to kill a man in his own house than in a field, because a man's house is his place of most secure refuge, it ought surely to be deemed more atrocious to destroy a fetus in the womb before it has come to light.[20]

For almost two thousand years the Church Eastern, Roman, and Protestant forthrightly taught Scripture's condemnation of spilling the man's seed and taking potions to obstruct pregnancy and childbearing. But why was there such unity on this issue among Christians of past generations? The answer is simple. Our fathers believed, as Scripture teaches, that "children are a gift of the LORD," and "the fruit of the womb is a reward." And they could not bear the thought of destroying or even preventing one of God's greatest gifts, nor of disregarding God's blessed commands to be fruitful and multiply.

But today, most Christian husbands and wives don't hesitate to prevent the gift of children in their lovemaking. And to make matters worse, we often accomplish that prevention by using methods of contraception that prevent childbirth by killing our little ones in the womb.

So what should we do?

For some readers, there must be repentance.

As a pastor, I am privileged to receive believers' confessions of sin. And I am aware that every church has mothers and fathers who have intentionally killed their babies, and without any confusion that what they were doing was murder. This is terribly sad. When some have confessed, it has been my privilege to assure them (and you) that this sin, too, is under the blood of Jesus Christ. King David murdered Uriah.

---

20. John Calvin, comments on Exodus 21:22ff (1563), trans. Charles William Bingham (1852), in *Harmony of the Law*, vol. 3, The Ages Digital Library Commentary (Books for the Ages, 1998), 32.

He was later confronted by the prophet Nathan, which led him to confess his sin and receive God's forgiveness:

> Deliver me from bloodguiltiness, O God, the God
>   of my salvation;
> Then my tongue will joyfully sing of Your
>   righteousness.   (Ps. 51:14)

Make David's humble plea your own. Throw yourself on God's mercy, believing always that we serve the God who alone forgives sins.

What about readers who killed a child unintentionally (through misunderstanding the Pill, for example)? Sadly, this does not remove your guilt. Whether or not we intended bloodshed, many of us have blood on our hands. If you have used a form of contraception that occasionally is abortive, that is sin. Take your sin to God.

What about truly non-abortive contraception?

I am convinced there are circumstances in which contraception is necessary to protect the mother and her family. We won't go into a discussion of such circumstances, but I have responded to requests for pastoral counsel from several couples by agreeing it would be wise to prevent further pregnancies. In these cases it was because of threats to the physical well-being of the mother, and that threat was neither hypothetical nor trivial.

On the other hand, many pastors don't hesitate to endorse any and every method of child prevention short of surgical abortion. One friend of mine publicly teaches that it is proper to use contraception to facilitate a couple's career as missionaries. Another friend, also a pastor, says couples should have no more children than they can "educate well." The publisher of *Christianity Today* once rejected an article I submitted on

God's blessing of children, telling me he thought one of his columnists was able to make a greater contribution to the kingdom of God through his writing because he and his wife had no children.

You may ask whether doing Christian work in a foreign country, giving our children a quality education, or being a famous writer are legitimate justifications for turning off God's blessings of children in our lovemaking. The answer is no.

To be honest, I think the church may have been better off without the books of the writer whose name the publisher mentioned to me. Too, I have expressed serious concern to my pastor friend that I think we (he and I, at least) need to repent of our idolatry of education. And concerning Christian couples who fly to another country to tell the souls there about Jesus, do we really want one of the main messages they take with them to be their childlessness? We already have the United Nations, USAID, and Planned Parenthood promoting contraception, birth control, and abortion. Do they need the church's help?

Yes, I believe there are rare situations where couples should use contraception. But let's not give our support to what Chesterton called "the modern and morbid weaknesses of always sacrificing the normal to the abnormal."[21] It may be that particular challenges of particular families lead a husband and wife to consider using contraception when it is not the physical life of the mother at stake. After searching their conscience and prayer, they believe God is leading them to close off the mother's womb, but this is the *exception*.

If this is indeed the reader's situation in his or her marriage, may I make a couple recommendations? First, find

---

21. G. K. Chesterton, *The Superstition of Divorce* (ch. 3) (John Lane Co., 1920), 48.

a godly physician you can discuss your situation with and receive biblical counsel from. (These are private matters, and so I don't recommend talking to just anyone.) Respect your physician, listening carefully and prayerfully, and yet don't take their advice blindly. If your Christian physician recommends the use of contraception, go to your pastor or an elder and talk it all over with him. Finally, be careful to use some barrier method, one which entirely prevents the union of sperm and egg, and not any method which functions—even secondarily—by preventing the implantation of a conceived baby in his mother's womb. And remember, no method of contraception is one hundred percent effective, so if God decides to give you another child while you are doing your best to avoid it, submit to His will and welcome your child with joy, trusting our heavenly Father to care for your expanded household.

We've come this far without talking much about the reasons a couple might be tempted to forgo children altogether. Of course, there's pure selfishness. But beyond that, our wicked world makes the idea of children feel increasingly challenging, to say the least.

Until the last half of the twentieth century, the world was structured around assuring that one breadwinner could earn a wage sufficient to support a full-time mother caring for a houseful of children. Then, in the last quarter of the twentieth century, we threw that away. Now mothers are expected to provide a second household income, and it's become difficult for families to get by without that second wage.

Then there's the grave injustice perpetrated by our governing authorities requiring Christians to pay thousands of dollars a year in taxes to support government education,

5 WHAT ABOUT BIRTH CONTROL?

while that education grows ever more antagonistic towards the Christian faith. Then, too, we have burdensome booster seat regulations that do almost nothing to lower child injuries and fatalities, and yet that do make it difficult for parents to find affordable family transportation.[22]

Furthermore, we have legal threats to biblical corporal punishment that keep parents in dread of child protective services. We have busybody neighbors who report a careful mother when she leaves a child in the front yard while she works around the side of the house. Christian fathers and mothers have their little ones taken from them by a government that judges the children to be endangered by their parents. And large families are more susceptible to these attacks, because one mother is not able to obsess over more than one or two children.

All that to say, it's understandable that many believers consider the cost of a fruitful marriage bed to be unsustainable. But isn't obeying God in this sinful world always costly? And isn't bearing children just another place where God requires us to trust in Him instead of trusting in earthly ease and prosperity? Haven't Christian mothers and fathers always had to exercise faith in God's kind provision for their family financially, physically, and spiritually?

But I hear the objections: *Are you saying we're supposed to have as many children as possible? Don't you think we've "multiplied" by now? Do you expect us to have children into our FORTIES?*

Such quibbling reminds me of similar questions about tithing: *Should I tithe on the net or the gross? How much giving*

---

22. See Steven D. Levitt and Joseph J. Doyle, "Evaluating the Effectiveness of Child Safety Seats and Seat Belts in Protecting Children from Injury," *Economic Inquiry* 48, no. 3 (July 2010): 521–536, https://doi.org/10.1111/j.1465-7295.2008.00170.x.

is enough? Are you saying I'm supposed to give EVERYTHING *to God?*

These questions come from a stingy heart. They are motivated not by a desire to please God, but by a desire to toe the line of *saying* we've obeyed God without actually having to exercise faith.

We are so very much like the rich young ruler in Matthew 19:16–23, who came to Jesus asking, "Teacher, what good thing shall I do that I may obtain eternal life?" We want to be able to do one good deed, to check one manageable box of righteousness, in order to get God's approval.

Jesus replies, "Keep the commandments."

That's more than we were hoping for, so we want to know specifics: "Which ones?"

"You shall not commit murder; You shall not commit adultery; You shall not steal; You shall not bear false witness; Honor your father and mother; and You shall love your neighbor as yourself."

We tell Jesus we've done a pretty good job of keeping those. And yet, we know in our hearts that we're still missing something, so we ask, "What am I still lacking?"

And Jesus smashes our self-righteousness: "If you wish to be complete, go and sell your possessions and give to the poor, and you will have treasure in heaven; and come, follow Me."

How did the rich young ruler respond to Jesus saying this? "He went away grieving; for he was one who owned much property." This poor man wanted it both ways. He wanted to be able to keep his great worldly wealth *and* have God's blessing. But Jesus says you can't serve God and wealth (Matt. 6:24). And that's why "it is hard for a rich man to enter the kingdom of heaven" (Matt. 19:23).

In our heart of hearts, many of us might admit we prefer a nice house, job security, fancy vacations, new cars, a summer place, a remodeled kitchen, or a boat over allowing God to bless us with children. But when we think biblically and decide this issue by faith, we come to realize that turning off God's gift of fruitfulness is incredibly expensive. Sure, we may have fuller bank accounts and less anxiety about what people think of us, but what about the emotional and spiritual costs of putting off fatherhood and motherhood? Of denying our wife the joy of a fruitful womb and a house full of children? And, ultimately, what will we say to God? He is the one who designed the marriage bed to be fruitful. Will we bury this treasure from our heavenly Father, complaining that He is a harsh taskmaster?[23]

Remember Jesus' warning:

> Do not store up for yourselves treasures on earth, where moth and rust destroy, and where thieves break in and steal. But store up for yourselves treasures in heaven, where neither moth nor rust destroys, and where thieves do not break in or steal; for where your treasure is, there your heart will be also. (Matt. 6:19–21)

But what do children have to do with storing up treasure in Heaven?

The Bible tells us God unites the husband and wife "for the propagation of a godly seed" (Mal. 2:15). In other words, God makes us one because it is His will that we raise up Christian children who will trust in Jesus Christ and bring Him glory. As we obey God by faith, as we are fruitful and multiply, Christ's glory multiplies, God is pleased, and we reap the benefits of God's blessings. What greater treasure could we ask for?

---

23. See Matthew 25:24–25.

Both Matthew and Mark record Jesus' interaction with the rich young ruler immediately after their accounts of the disciples rebuking people who were bringing little children to Jesus. Do you remember Jesus' indignant response?

> Permit the children to come to Me; do not hinder them; for the kingdom of God belongs to such as these. Truly I say to you, whoever does not receive the kingdom of God like a child will not enter it at all. (Mark 10:13–15)

The kingdom of God belongs to little children. Do we think we're wiser than God? Are we sending little ones away because they're an inconvenience to us? Or will we exercise faith and welcome these gifts and rewards from God with open arms and hearts?

The last few years of his life, my father had much to be grateful for. He had books and speaking engagements. He was CEO of a publishing house. Christian leaders looked to him for counsel. He'd had a monthly column in an Evangelical magazine for twenty-five years. He was still married to his wife and they loved each other. But, in his final years Dad would regularly say his children gave him his greatest happiness. We were nothing special. And yet, looking back over his life, that was Dad's testimony.

Bearing and raising children is hard—very hard—but we can't afford not to do it, because those children become our treasure, and where our treasure is, there our hearts will be also. My dad was no anomaly. All fathers and mothers love their children—both the ones who are easy to raise and the ones who are not. God the Father put that love in our hearts, and we ought to follow it.

Mary Lee and I have been living without our children for

5 WHAT ABOUT BIRTH CONTROL?

about a decade now. When our youngest son left, we felt his absence. We have a large dining room table, and after Taylor's departure, Mary Lee continued to set the table. And there she and I sat eating each night, alone and bereft.

After a while I asked if we could sit at the kitchen island instead. Mary Lee asked why and I said, "I can't bear sitting there, just the two of us, with no children. It's depressing. I wouldn't notice as much if we just ate in the kitchen." So now, for the past eight years or so, we've been eating in the kitchen.

Meanwhile, God has blessed our children with scads of children of their own, so that Mary Lee and I now have twenty-nine grandchildren, and expect more. A few years ago a bunch of them needed to be driven somewhere, and I was nominated. I climbed high up into the driver's seat of my daughter's gargantuan van, the kids piled in, and we were off.

May I tell you something? Driving the grandkids in that van, I was the happiest I'd been in years. I smiled. We sang. I listened to their music. A half hour or so into the trip, I realized how pumped I was and wondered why.

Then it hit me. Children. Scads of them yakking and arguing and bragging, some kind and some not so kind, all together living lives given them by God. What gifts. What treasures. Such happiness. Such blessings.

Cynical readers might respond by pointing out I didn't have to change those kids' diapers and spank them and do their wash. All I was doing was sitting in the driver's seat for one trip.

True enough.

Still, what joy came that day, revisiting the happiness of fatherhood. All those years with all those children. Hard work, yes (and even harder for Mary Lee). But nothing in life compares to the joy of children. So said God, and I testify to you in all sincerity, so I have found, and so our children now find.

Reader, will you trust God? Will you give yourselves to fruitfulness? No greater joy will ever come to you and your wife, even as it comes with many sorrows. Your treasure will be laid up in Heaven where, one day, those children will join you in singing God's praises around His throne. There you all will live happily ever after.

CHAPTER 6
Leaving and Cleaving

For this reason a man shall leave his father
and his mother, and be joined to his wife;
and they shall become one flesh.

— Genesis 2:24

Marriage is no private Christian thing. At the very beginning God created man and woman. Then He ordained that a man shall leave his father and mother and be joined to his wife, becoming one flesh with her.

Before we open up the significance of these commands, a word about significance of creation commands in general.

God is our Creator. No man created himself. No woman created herself. God made us, and it's His prerogative to command us. "Does not the potter have a right over the clay?" (Rom. 9:21). God's authority over us does not come from our acknowledgment of His creating us, but from the simple fact that He did. Which means, those who deny that He made us are no less subject to His authority and commands than those who affirm it.

But it's tempting for us to act and speak as if God's laws apply only to those of us who are Christians, especially in the Western world which is presently so intent on trashing

God's authority and law. And it's true, acting and speaking this way—keeping our religion private and personal—saves us a lot of grief. Nowhere is this more enticing to us than the creation commands concerning sexuality and marriage.

Of course, there are commands in Scripture that apply specifically and only to God's people. Think of the Old Testament dietary laws. Think of the New Testament commands concerning baptism and the Lord's Supper. But God's creation laws of sexuality are not in this category. They are not limited to Christians alone.

Whether you're a Christian or an unbeliever, obeying God's truths of sexuality will bring you lifelong blessings and happiness, and forsaking those truths will bring judgment from God in this life and in the life to come. We know that these laws in particular apply to everyone because of Scripture's testimony that these creation commands were declared by God in the garden of Eden prior to the Fall. They were given to Adam, the father of all mankind, when all things were still in a state of perfection, and sin had corrupted nothing. For this reason they are not private truths, but universal laws binding on every man and woman everywhere and always.

What laws are we talking about?

- Marriage is to be lifelong monogamy: The two shall become one flesh.
- Marriage is to be heterosexual: A man shall be joined to his wife.
- Marriage is ordered by the husband's authority over his wife: Adam was created first, then Eve.

We must return to preaching and teaching these laws, not only to those in our families and churches, but also to Shiite Muslims, Buddhists, Marxists, Yale alumni, Romanians,

6 LEAVING AND CLEAVING

Zambians, Afghans, and (you guessed it) the Supreme Court of the United States.

Note that one of these commands is that the man shall leave his father and mother, and be joined to his wife. And the first thing to observe is that it's the man who is commanded to leave his father and mother. Why the man rather than the woman? Is the woman *not* to leave her father and mother?

No, this would be nonsensical. The wedding ceremony demonstrates the woman's departure in a very public way with the question, "Who gives this woman to be married to this man?" This is the transfer of authority from the father of the old household to the father of the new household. The bride's father answers, "I do," then kisses his daughter and joins her hand to the hand of the groom. She has left her father and mother to be joined to her husband.

But the man? Marriage ceremonies have no ritual of departure for grooms. Yet we recognize from the command recorded in Genesis 2 that leaving and cleaving is demanded of the groom. Which is actually a kindness to the bride, if you think about it. Since the wife is commanded by God to submit to her husband, the husband is in a good position to assure his wife leaves her father and mother. The wife, though, is not in as good a position to get her husband to leave his father and mother. But in His kindness, God Himself has given the husband this command from the very beginning. In other words, God's command protects the woman, lest her husband refuse to cut the apron strings and choose to cling to his mother more than to his wife. This would be tragic, so God commands the husband to cut the apron strings. He is to leave his father and mother. His father and mother are not to be allowed to undercut his new bride.

It used to be said America's greatest loves were the flag, apple pie, and motherhood. Back in high school my best friend made the mistake of saying something about another player's mother during a basketball game in gym class. I didn't hear what he said, so I was shocked to see my friend flying backward, landing hard on his rear end. If you want a long life, don't say anything about a man's mother.

Well, Jesus said something about His own mother, and He gave us an important lesson that applies to a man leaving father and mother. He was in a crowded house, and His mother and brothers couldn't get to Him. Stuck outside, they sent a message saying they wanted to see Him. Here's how Jesus responded:

> "Who is My mother and who are My brothers?" And stretching out His hand toward His disciples, He said, "Behold My mother and My brothers! For whoever does the will of My Father who is in heaven, he is My brother and sister and mother." (Matt. 12:48–50)

Jesus wasn't dismissive of His mother and brothers, but He did relegate them when a more important relationship (with His Father) was at stake. In a similar way, the well-being of our bride requires the relegation of our father and mother. Scripture could have simply said that a man shall be joined to his wife, but instead we husbands are specifically told to leave our father and mother. Our wife must not be added to our mother's household. She must have her own household headed by her husband who has turned from his mother to his wife.

I remember staying the night with a single friend of ours who had been in our congregation but had recently moved back home to New York City. He was Chinese and lived with his family in a three-story row house. His room was up on the second floor, and we spent the evening talking. He had a room to himself and it was clear he was well taken care of.

6 LEAVING AND CLEAVING

During the conversation, I asked about his family. He said his father and mother lived there, as well as his grandmother and a number of other family members—aunts and uncles, and their families. But, he added, he had his own bedroom because he was his grandmother's favorite.

His grandmother? What did she have to do with it? I asked.

He explained that in Chinese culture the father and his bride move in with the father's mother. She rules the roost, runs the household, and presides as top dog, even down to choosing which bedroom everyone gets. Somewhat sheepishly, he admitted his grandmother had always spoiled him.

This is no argument against extended families living together. However, it is shameful for a grandmother to be the head of an extended household, including her son and his wife. This is not biblical, nor is it right for her to use her authority over the men to give preferential treatment to her grandson.

Another temptation for husbands not to leave and cleave (as the King James Version puts it) is the guilt of broken marriages and homes. Thirty years ago in *The Closing of the American Mind*, Professor Allan Bloom warned of the terrible toll divorce was taking on his students who were children of divorced parents:

> A large measure of their enthusiasm has been extinguished and replaced by self-protectiveness.... More than any students I have known, they evoke pity. They are indeed victims.
>
> An additional factor in the state of these students' souls is the fact that they have undergone therapy. They have been told how to feel and what to think about themselves by psychologists who are paid by their parents to make everything

> work out as painlessly as possible for the parents, as part of no-fault divorce. If ever there was a conflict of interest, this is it. There are big bucks for therapists in divorce.... Psychologists are the sworn enemies of guilt.[1]

Sadly, what was true thirty-five years ago is more true today. Not that the divorce rate has increased. Since Bloom, the divorce rate has actually decreased, but that's largely because of the decrease in marriages in general. And with that comes the drastic increase in the proportion of children born and raised without fathers. This causes great damage, and we know it. God has written His law on our hearts, and mothers who forgo husbands know the destruction this causes their children, just as fathers who abandon their children's mother know it. And no matter how hard the therapists work, the burden of guilt passed on to children from their parents doesn't just go away. Our children don't grow up confident, but timid and fearful, and guilt is everywhere stunting their emotional and spiritual growth.

This guilt takes a heavy toll on the groom and bride setting out to build their household. It does so in a variety of ways, but most commonly through mothers and fathers manipulating their adult children as they try to reclaim the years the locust has eaten. The mother who has been abandoned by her husband, whether emotionally or through separation or divorce, often cannot keep herself from looking to her son for the emotional intimacy she's lost, and this continues into marriage and adulthood. Which is to say, this mother becomes a very clear and present danger to her son's wife.

She may oppose the woman from the first, doing everything she can to obstruct any engagement or marriage. She may complain about the woman's hair or clothing or cooking, hoping her son returns to his mother who knows the right way to make chicken soup. She may simply whine and cry and throw herself a pity party.

As many wives find out too late, marriage to such a son is suicidal. There is no room for cleaving because there's no room for leaving. His father abandoned his mother and it's his life's work to heal her emotional wounds. After all, what is a wife compared to a mother? Did his wife give birth to him? Did she diaper and clothe him? Did she nurse him? How can she claim to love him anything near as much as his mama loves him? Wives come and go, but men have only one mother who bore, birthed, and nursed them.

But mothers aren't the only culprits. The husband must leave his father too, and fathers can manipulate their grown children in similar ways. As a pastor, I've counseled adult children whose absent fathers were trying to reestablish relationships after those children finally reached the age of majority and moved away from their mother. (Since mothers usually have custody, dads often give up on a relationship with their children.)

The net result? The "child" might be thirty or forty years old now, married with four or five kids of his own, yet still having to negotiate his way between a bitter father and mother who, in their sixties and seventies, are trying to get everything they can from their children emotionally in order to justify their marital dissolution, desperately working to make up for years of neglect and abandonment.

The sins of parents—whether fornication, homosexual partnership, adultery, or divorce—mound up an almost insurmountable weight of guilt that destroys children even to the second and third generation. Be on guard against the exploitation of this guilt by the pleas, tears, anger, and manipulation of your mother and father. Husbands, don't make your wife fight your mother or father in defense of herself and

THE HELPFUL MARRIAGE BOOK

her children. It is your duty to protect your wife from this danger—and not because she forces you to do so, but rather because God commands you to do so.

You are not responsible for your parents' divorce, and you can't heal their wounded hearts. This is the work of God. He forgives sin, so leave it to Him to accomplish through the preaching of the Gospel. Don't try to short-circuit the pain of a bad conscience, thinking you yourself may heal it if you can figure out whose house to visit with your children for Thanksgiving and Christmas.

There's another challenge for children of divorced parents. Such children often have never experienced the beauty of a loving relationship between husband and wife. What they have experienced is fighting and, in between the fights, a joyless relationship. This forms their own imagination of what their future marriage will be like. Commonly, then, fearful of marriage, they choose unstable relationships. Or worse, they get married with an escape plan in their mind, just in case "things go bad." The point is, young people especially need role models of happy marriages. Church members should be sensitive to these fears and invite children of broken marriages to spend time with families whose marriages are truly happy (though perhaps also difficult).

Those of you from broken homes: Forget the past and press on to the high calling you yourself have received from our Lord Jesus. Don't return to your sad and guilt-ridden childhood home, but build the beautiful marriage and home your heavenly Father has now given you. Doing so is not heartless and cruel. You are *not* responsible for healing your mother or father. You *are* responsible for leaving them and cleaving to your own flesh, your husband or wife and all the children God has given you.

When we lived in Wisconsin, there was a handsome father

6 LEAVING AND CLEAVING

and beautiful mother in our community who had a tidy and profitable dairy farm, one which their own handsome son and beautiful daughter-in-law would eventually inherit. That was where everything was headed, and what a wonderful day that would be—from father to son to son.

But the thing was, every single morning following chores, this handsome son would sit and have coffee with his beautiful mother. And every one of those wonderful mornings mother and son sat and talked over their coffee, the beautiful daughter-in-law was back home feeding and clothing her own beautiful and beloved children. Daddy was gone, Mama would explain. He was having coffee with his *own* mommy. After the years passed, the handsome son and his beautiful wife divorced. And no, not all subsequence is consequence, but in this case, my wife and I have no doubt.

Another man—brilliant and well respected, an only child—had a mother who was the recipient of her son's filial devotion. He visited her every Sunday. He saw to her every need. He was the perfectly dutiful son, but sadly, he was also childless and divorced. He and I grew close over a couple years, and one day he stated matter-of-factly that his mother had broken up his marriage. I didn't pry, but I did remember.

A few years passed and this man remarried, but his mother refused to acknowledge the marriage. She wouldn't see his new wife, and in time, there was enough strain on the marriage that his wife asked my wife and me for help. We began to meet with this couple, but our marriage counseling ground to a halt as soon as we broached the subject of this man's mother. Reminding him privately that he'd told me his mother had broken up his first marriage, I asked if he wanted her to break up his second one also. Sadly, that was the end of our counseling. Mommy came first, wife second, and the pastor who pointed out this sin was cut off.

Let us remember the words of our Lord:

> From the beginning of creation, God made them male and female. For this reason a man shall leave his father and mother, and the two shall become one flesh; so they are no longer two, but one flesh. What therefore God has joined together, let no man separate. (Mark 10:6–8)

What therefore God has joined together, let no mother or father separate.

May God give you wisdom for your departure. Your extrication. And remember, it is not the wife's responsibility to whine about it. It's the man's joy to leave and cleave. Husbands, may He give you a loving sensitivity to the vulnerability of your wife and the children she presents you—children whose well-being depends on your obedience to this command of God.

One final thought: If you are not the young husband, but the older father, and your wife is the mother manipulating her son, that's on you. Give your daughter-in-law and grandchildren the wonderful gift of bringing this sin to an end. Help your son by saying no to your wife.

CHAPTER 7
You Need the Church

The Jerusalem above is free; she is our mother.

—Galatians 4:26

Our marriage began with a search for a church. After our honeymoon, we had moved to Madison, Wisconsin, and began to visit Sunday morning worship services at Bible-believing churches. We were repenting of our sin and didn't want to start married life cut off from the people of God and the preaching of His Word, so we searched and searched, but found no home suitable for us.

One church had an altar call at the end of each sermon, and that wasn't what we wanted. Another church had this or that we didn't like, and so it went, until one Sunday afternoon as I was reading Dietrich Bonhoeffer's little book *Life Together*. I was astounded that he was talking to, and rebuking, us. I called out for Mary Lee, and she came and lay down on the carpet in our hallway where I had been reading. I read to her:

> Innumerable times a whole Christian community has broken down because it had sprung from a wish dream. The

serious Christian, set down for the first time in a Christian community, is likely to bring with him a very definite idea of what Christian life together should be and to try to realize it. But God's grace speedily shatters such dreams. Just as surely as God desires to lead us to a knowledge of genuine Christian fellowship, so surely must we be overwhelmed by a great disillusionment with others, with Christians in general, and, if we are fortunate, with ourselves.

By sheer grace, God will not permit us to live even for a brief period in a dream world. . . . Every human wish dream that is injected into the Christian community is a hindrance to genuine community and must be banished if genuine community is to survive. He who loves his dream of a community more than the Christian community itself becomes a destroyer of the latter, even though his personal intentions may be ever so honest and earnest and sacrificial.

God hates visionary dreaming; it makes the dreamer proud and pretentious. The man who fashions a visionary ideal of community demands that it be realized by God, by others, and by himself. He enters the community of Christians with his demands, sets up his own law, and judges the brethren and God himself accordingly. He stands adamant, a living reproach to all others in the circle of brethren. He acts as if he is the creator of the Christian community, as if his dream binds men together. When things do not go his way, he calls the effort a failure. When his ideal picture is destroyed, he sees the community going to smash. So he becomes, first an accuser of his brethren, then an accuser of God, and finally the despairing accuser of himself.[1]

As I write today, the church is divided over Covid and people are switching churches so they can be with people that agree with them. This will change, and not too long from now it will be something else. I've lived through a lot of these things people use to leave churches over. This isn't a family-centered church. People here don't homeschool. No one here has any of their kids in public school. They use wine for the Lord's Supper. They use grape juice for the Lord's Supper. They have women serving communion. They don't have any women serving communion. People wear masks in worship.

As Bonhoeffer put it, "The man who fashions a visionary ideal of community demands that it be realized by God, by others, and by himself. He enters the community of Christians with his demands, sets up his own law, and judges the brethren and God himself accordingly."

Is this you?

Mary Lee and I realized Bonhoeffer had our number, so we repented. We didn't think to ourselves, "Where does this guy get off, thinking he has the right to speak to us about our sin?" We repented. We began to love a truth succinctly stated by the Early Church father Cyprian: "He can no longer have God for his Father, who has not the Church for his mother."[2]

Martin Luther writes:

> Therefore he who would find Christ must first find the Church. How should we know where Christ and his faith were, if we did not know where his believers are? And he who would know anything of Christ must not trust himself nor build a bridge to heaven by his own reason; but he must go to the Church, attend and ask her.
>
> Now the Church is not wood and stone, but the company of believing people; one must hold to them, and see how they believe, live and teach; they surely have Christ in their midst. For outside of the Christian church there is no truth, no Christ, no salvation.[3]

THE HELPFUL MARRIAGE BOOK

Protestant church confessions have repeated this truth for centuries: "The visible Church ... is the Kingdom of the Lord Jesus Christ, the house and family of God, out of which there is no ordinary possibility of salvation."[4]

We must embrace this truth as married couples. If the Lord is to be the Builder of our house, we must love and obey Him, giving ourselves and our family to His things and His people. We must not trust ourselves to build a godly marriage and home by our own reason, independently following our own inner lights. Rather, we must go to the church, ask her help, and listen to her as she cares for us through her teaching, preaching, and pastoral care.

As Mary Lee and I read Bonhoeffer, we realized we should be grateful for the church and her care. We shouldn't judge her. Thus we chose one church and stuck with her until, several years later, we moved from Madison to Boulder where we joined First Presbyterian Church; and then to Boston for seminary where we gave ourselves to First Presbyterian Church in South Hamilton the three years we lived there.

The churches in Madison, Boulder, and Boston had weaknesses, but all three of them were blessings to us our first years of marriage as we built our household. How?

They loved us. They cared for us. They prayed for us. They taught us. They preached to us. They prayed for us. They fed us. They admonished us. They prayed for us. They encouraged us. They served us the Lord's Supper and fed us the Word. And did I mention they prayed for us?

We remember many meals we ate in restaurants and in the homes of church members at each of the three churches. Reformed Church in Madison hired us to clean the church and allowed us to care for their high school children by leading their youth group. First Pres in Boulder hired us, putting me to work teaching an adult Sunday school class, helping train their lay counselors, teaching junior high students, starting a small group, and serving in other ways on their pastoral staff. As we left, they affirmed our pastoral gifts, taking us under care and supporting us financially through seminary. First Pres in South Hamilton allowed me to serve a pastoral internship among them, meeting each week with the pastor and leading worship; and also provided me my first opportunity to preach. And of course we happily remember things like Prof. Charles Schauffele getting up early each Tuesday morning and driving to the church-house where he prepared breakfast for the men who came to the early morning Bible study and prayer group. What kindnesses these churches showed us!

But let's get back to prayer. What would Mary Lee and I have done without confessing ours sins and having brothers and sisters in Christ pray for us? All weddings are followed by difficulties, and Mary Lee and I were no different. Every marriage is between two sinners. Both of us were stubborn. Both of us were feminists. Both of us were selfish. I had a temper, and Mary Lee wasn't submissive. Both of us had long been flirts, and that was dangerous at the start of marriage. You don't just turn off patterns of sin once you're married, and although flirting is always sin, flirting in the first years of marriage in particular can be fatal to your marriage and your soul.

Mary Lee and I were counter-cultural punks (much like hipsters today). I'd seen an old sailor standing outside his store in downtown San Diego. He seemed a real man and I decided to get my ear pierced so I could look the real man too. Mary Lee worked for a jewelry store in San Francisco's Cannery, piercing customers' ears, and one day she pierced her nose and started wearing a diamond stud. I drove an old VW Bug. Mary Lee had a perm, and my hair was down to my shoulders. We were pieces of work, yet our churches loved and accepted us. And prayed and prayed for us.

Which brings us back, again, to prayer. Unless the Lord builds the house, the builders labor in vain. So pray. Without ceasing. Never stop confessing your sins to other believers and asking them to pray for you. You want God to build your marriage and household, so plead for His help and get others to plead with Him in your behalf.

This is very simple and very hard. Mary Lee and I found a prayer group that met each week in Covenant Presbyterian Church there in Madison. It was led by a godly older couple named Elmer and Mitzi McMurry. Eight to ten of us attended faithfully each week, and although all of us believed in prayer, it was hard to be the dirty ones who had real prayer requests for real sins each week. All the other requests were for things like the healing of the gammy leg of somebody's neighbor or aunt, or someone asking us to pray "that things at work would get better."

We knew the rest of the prayer group saw us as their project. I remember being tempted to resent the absence of any confessions or requests for prayer for sins coming from anyone else, but God directed us to keep going, to keep confessing our sins and keep asking for prayer, humbling as it was, and we obeyed. The people of God there loved us, and we saw God answer their prayers for us as we began to grow and to put some sins behind us, moving on to concentrate on others.

That's the Christian life, isn't it?

Sanctification is humiliating and painful; sanctification is lifelong, and what joy it is to begin ever so slowly to grow in our family likeness to the Church's Bridegroom, our Lord Jesus. In His Word God warns that sanctification can never be separated from salvation. You must have it because Scripture commands us to "pursue sanctification," then adds the warning, "without which no one will see the Lord" (Heb. 12:14). No, sanctification doesn't save us, yet without it no man will see the Lord.

From the very beginning of marriage, pursue sanctification together by fighting your sin together. And for this fighting there is no substitute for the church of Jesus Christ. Her feeding. Her admonishments. Her worship. Her preaching. Her cleansing through the water of baptism and the milk of the Word. Her fellowship around the Lord's Table. God Himself has appointed that the care you and your family need will only come from Him through the worship, fellowship, and care of the church. He has appointed her to be your mother.

This is why the true Christian would rather miss the Super Bowl than Lord's Day worship. Even if he's dying of cancer, the believing man will go to church, joining God's people in worship in anticipation of that day almost upon him when he will be gathered with all the saints, praising God together with His holy angels.

Faithful reader, you may have been raised to think that some people need the church and other people of superior breeding and moral virtue don't. That some people need the rebukes of the pastors, elders, and older women, but that the better sort of people live above such dependency, making it mostly on their own (except maybe for baptisms, weddings, and funerals). They're on a largely self-directed journey to Heaven. They know how to manage their own finances (certainly better than the church manages finances). They know how to run their own businesses. They know how to run their own home and family, so they certainly don't need any man's help with their soul. They certainly don't need advice raising their children. They don't sin, so they don't need anyone to confess their sin to and ask for prayer from. They don't doubt. They aren't bitter. They don't steal. They have their lust under control. They don't argue. They don't even get angry (except at things everyone should be angry about).

Have you noticed how we despise authority today? We all want churches with pastors who stay in the pulpit. We don't want pastors in our living room. We want elders in the board room but not in our kitchen. And we don't need any older woman speaking to us about our motherhood or housekeeping or immodesty.

Those who think this way are simply fools.

Every believer desperately needs the church on Sundays, Mondays, Tuesdays, Wednesdays, Thursdays, Fridays, and Saturdays. It's possible some readers think I write this because I'm a pastor, and if people don't come to church, I don't get to collect the offering.

Nope. Without the church we die.

Now, one last thing before we close this chapter.

Years back I heard an older pastor say the best predictor of perseverance in Christian faith was a lifelong commitment to one church. Now of course there are times when we have to leave a church and find another. Sometimes we move. Sometimes the church moves—into heresy, that is. But putting such occasions aside, think of all the times you have wanted to leave your church because you were bitter or angry or hurt or ashamed at your sin being seen and known by the assembly of believers—or maybe just seen and known by the elders and pastors. Think of all the times you have wanted to leave because people in your congregation don't agree with you on gluten or breadmaking or masks.

Don't do it. Do not jeopardize your own soul and the souls

of your wife and children to save face. Do not jeopardize your salvation to satisfy your own preferences on secondary matters like frequency of communion, Psalm singing, or the use of musical instruments in leading the praise of the people of God.

Since hearing that older pastor make this observation of the connection between church commitment and spiritual life, I've seen it prove true over and over again, and now I add my own agreement to it. Sometimes Mary Lee and I go through the list of those who have left the church angry, ashamed, bitter, proud, or condemning, and we begin to name their children who are living in flagrant sin without any fruit of true faith. We don't do it often because it's sad. Often one of the elders or pastors warned the father or mother of the consequences of their pride, bitterness, and judgmentalism, but to no avail. It's shocking how many of these families have gone through three, four, and five other churches after leaving ours.

The only currency of church life is forgiveness, and let's face it, almost always it is a refusal to receive forgiveness or to give it that causes us to leave a church. This must not be. God has forgiven you—how can you refuse to forgive your brother or sister in Christ? How can you refuse to confess your sins to man when you say you've confessed them to God?

If you have left a church in bitterness, consider this warning from our Lord:

> If you forgive others for their transgressions, your heavenly Father will also forgive you. But if you do not forgive others, then your Father will not forgive your transgressions.
> (Matt. 6:14–15)

In a previous book on the church, I wrote:

> If you have trouble loving the Church; if a church has failed you in the past and you refuse to love and give yourself to the Church now; if you talk contemptuously about "the institutional church"; if you refuse to become a church member; if you say you won't join any church because you submit to Jesus alone; if you attend a megachurch where you're neither known nor loved; if you attend a church where the pastor gives a lecture and knows no more about you than your dental hygienist does; then don't lie to yourself. You don't love the Church any more than a wife who, hurt by her husband, spends the rest of her life refusing intimacy with him.
>
> When we turn from intimacy with the Church, we must realize our Lord Himself has not done so. Will you repent and begin to give yourself to the Church?[5]

Now then, unless the Lord builds the house, they labor in vain who build it. You cannot build your marriage and home without Jesus. He has given you His church for that help. Do not despise her.

She is your mother.

Chapter 8
Fight the Good Fight

Be angry, and yet do not sin; do not let the sun go down on your anger.

— Ephesians 4:26

It was clear two of the souls under my care were committing adultery. It was the way they looked at each other and touched each other. It was the way they did not look at their own spouses or show affection for them.

One day the woman committing adultery asked to meet. During our time together, I spotted a lead-in and took it, saying, "Since you dislike your husband so much, who *are* you turning to for intimacy?" After the initial shock and anger, it all came out. Later that evening, we met with her and her husband, and she confessed her sin to him.

The next day, we met with the other couple for the man's confession to his wife. The response of the wife who was being cheated on was raw in its fury. After a few minutes firing questions at her cowed husband, she turned to him and asked pathetically, "But why?" After a pause, she softly said to no one in particular, "But we *never* fight."

Later, after they had left, I asked Mary Lee, "What's wrong with *us*? *We* fight."

Mary Lee was primed for it: "Of course they don't fight. They don't *care* about each other."

This lesson stuck with us. Ever since, Mary Lee and I have understood how necessary marital disagreement is, and what it accomplishes.

Another couple we knew liked to say they never argued. But then, years later, we sat with this couple as they both confessed sexual sin they had committed against each other, but had never talked about.

Another couple had the most clean and perfect children and home. Of course they never fought. Having grown up in a family where several of my brothers died in childhood, I kept it in mind that this couple had lost a child years earlier. As we grew close to them, it became clear that, after their son died, their marriage became brittle. They never talked about him, and it seemed to me they had failed to do the hard work of grieving together.

The work of mourning the death of a child is extremely difficult for father and mother, not to mention brothers and sisters. And yet, accusations, guilt, depression, and fights are the necessary paths we all travel back to health. If we put this work off or avoid it, intimacy and love are replaced by sins against one another, including (but not limited to) rigidity and perfectionism. If, however, we walk those paths of conflict, the fruit is tender and deep. Grieving not only heals us as father and mother, but it creates freedom for the healing of our sons and daughters who also need to grieve.

All of this to say, avoidance of pain and conflict in marriage and family relations is natural, but it produces bitter fruit. On the other hand, if we allow pain to do its work, it produces trust in God's sovereignty, and peace in our homes. If you never go through the ugliness and pain of a good fight, you never experience the sweetness of forgiveness. Have you ever noticed how sweet it is to make love after a fight with your husband or wife? The lows and highs of marriage are intimately related.

This is because marriage is between sinners, and so it is filled with sins. *Every* marriage. Every Christian marriage, too.

Of course sin is sad, but it only makes things worse if we deny what's going on. Living together in anything approaching honesty requires two sinners to talk about their sin. And then, ironically, it's hard to talk about your sins without sinning even more during that conversation. But we must do it if we want to grow.

Christian marriage is between two sinners, both of whom need sanctification. The husband and wife must not be prissy about this, denying the necessity of this work in one another. Couples have the privilege of working with the Holy Spirit as they call one another to holiness. But yes, even the best husband gets irritated when he is called to this work by his wife. Maybe even some wives are less than overjoyed when they're called to this work by their husbands.

Conflict is necessary for the pursuit of sanctification. But if we're going to fight, we need to fight well. So let's go over some helpful things to know and do when we have fights.

First, pay attention to Scripture's command, "Do not let the sun go down on your anger."

We have a warm memory of a couple named Ray and Beth Knighton greeting us in the receiving line following our wedding and stopping long enough to say, "You two call us any time you need help. And remember, don't *ever* go to bed angry." (They gave us pillows for a wedding gift.) We needed that and continue to remember those few words as a gift of love from Mr. and Mrs. Knighton given (along with pillows) at the threshold of our married life.

And yet, some of our worst fights happen around midnight when you can't even keep your thoughts straight and emotions are out of control. Someone needs to break the tension and say, "It's too late for us to continue this. Let's stop and see if we can't figure it out in the morning."

Don't fight late into the night. Have a rule you won't fight after, say, 10 PM. Agree that any fight that remains unresolved by 10 PM will come under a cease-and-desist order. Nighttime is for sleeping, and no one who is angry sleeps very well.

So stop. Maybe you can't actually go through apologies and forgiveness at that late hour, but regardless, do not let the sun go down on your anger. In the morning things never seem as bad as they did the night before. It's usually easier to resolve the conflict in the morning.

Next rule: Be angry, but sin not.

In marriage you will get angry. What you must not do in your anger is sin. Many times the anger itself will not be sin, but what the anger causes you to do will be. People often think any anger is sin, but that's not true. The Spirit of God commands us, "Be angry, and yet do not sin." In other words, anger itself can be righteous.

Your husband is driving and stares at a young woman in a sundress walking across the street. This angers you, and that's good and right. But don't turn to your teenage daughter in the back seat and say, "Your dad thinks she's hot." That's letting your anger run away with you. You should not cultivate your daughter's disrespect for her father.

Pray, asking the Holy Spirit to keep you from sinning in your anger. Have faith that He will answer your prayer.

In marriage counseling, we have worked with couples whose fights escalate into the husband or wife having temper tantrums with name-calling, smashing dishes, punching walls, slamming doors, threatening divorce, and storming out of the house. In some of these marriages, such sins have become a pattern which the gentler spouse dreads, but thinks there's nothing to be done about it.

Wrong. This is not a tolerable state of affairs for the spouse or any children in the home. It is not godly to leave such a sinner in his bondage—his pattern of sin. "Be angry and sin not" is God's command to us, so we obey that command, not explaining our temper tantrums with cheap excuses like, "Dad had a temper, and I inherited it."

Readers who think their wife or husband is incapable of being angry without sinning may find it helpful to stop for a moment and think about where and when their spouse has tantrums and explodes in fury. I was talking to a husband once, and he lamented his frequent rages at home, but claimed he was powerless against them. They just happened and that was that.

Sitting there listening, it occurred to me this man was in perfect control of his anger. The proof was that, for years, he had been holding down an office job in a large corporation. Human resources wouldn't have put up with him if he'd ever even once lost his temper at work the way he regularly did at home. Why was it only at home that he drank himself into oblivion, cursing and shouting? Why did he rail against his wife and children, but never against his boss and coworkers?

The obvious answer is that he knew his supervisor at work wouldn't put up with it for even one second. At work he'd be fired, so he kept his mouth and temper under control during the day, only unleashing them against his wife and children at home. It wasn't that he had a bad wife and children, but a good boss and coworkers. He knew his wife would just take it. She would not ask her elders, pastors, or any older woman of the church for help.

Don't make excuses for your own or your spouse's sinful

anger, whether that sin is curses, slammed doors, broken dishes, or slinking away to look at porn. You are a moral agent. All men and women are. God made each of us responsible for the sins we commit, including the sins we commit in anger. Fathers, confess your sin and go to the elders for prayer and healing.

Now let's spend some time looking at ways we can make sure our conflict in marriage is productive.

Of course, there are many good rules for communication that minimize conflict and hostility. Send "I" rather than "you" messages. Avoid the words "never" and "always." Talk about how you feel without doing so in an accusatory way. Don't make assumptions. Learn to recognize body language. Be willing to state directly what you think you'd find helpful in the future, rather than having a hissy fit over the past. Repeat back to your wife or husband what they just said, doing it in a way that shows you understand and have sympathy for their position. These and other rules for good communication are very helpful and can be effective in bringing peace back to your relationship. Learn and use them.

But let's talk specifically about the three big fights in marriage. They used to say these were conflicts about money, sex, and children. (More recently, people have changed it to money, sex, and maybe "free time," "extended family," or "chores," but that's a sign of our degraded culture.) Let's tackle these one by one.

Money

They say you can see what someone loves by watching what he spends money on. The miser hoards his money while the prodigal son spends it quickly, trying to buy friends and lovers through parties, food, drugs, booze, and entertainment. But most of us aren't out-and-out misers or prodigals, so it's a little harder to tease things out. That's where the wife or husband comes in. Usually they know what we're spending money on, and if they don't like it, they raise the issue with us. That's how many of our fights over money start.

One or the other of us keeps the bank account and notices balances are low. One or the other of us makes payments on the credit cards and watches the debt grow. We watch our spouse work on refinancing our mortgage and find out it's going to be a cash-out loan. Our credit scores are getting worse. We're forced to make late payments to the dentist and pediatrician. We miss our student loan payments. Then three of these things happen within a few weeks of each other and the fight is on.

Maybe the wife spends money on haircuts, clothes for herself and the kids, eating out, home decor, and coffee. Maybe the husband spends money on his pickup truck, guns, fishing trips, or buying cigarettes and lottery tickets. Don't make a federal case of his or her financial decisions. Instead, make a peaceable life with this husband or wife you vowed to love and cherish until death separates you. But how?

Three simple recommendations.

First, get help. Someone outside your marriage can say things without arousing the same level of irritation and anger as you yourself saying them to your husband or wife. So get help. Early. Get help with a stingy spouse who loves money and lives in greed. Get help with a spendthrift spouse who loves money and lives in greed. Financial help is easy to get. The question is whether both of you want to listen.

Ask your spouse to join you once or twice a week listening to Dave Ramsey's radio advice, or read his book *Complete Guide to Money* together. Or find help in the church. We have a man in our congregation who is a financial planner. He and his wife meet regularly with couples from church to help them get started on budgeting. You may not have someone in your church who is a professional, but surely there is an older couple willing to meet with you to discuss your difficulties.

Second, share everything. Since the two of you are one; since God made you one; since God joined the two of you together, one flesh; jump into that oneness with both feet financially. As much as it depends on you, guard your money from belonging to one or the other of you. Use the ownership of your bank accounts and assets to lead you together, rather than apart. Although there are special circumstances in some marriages where all assets should not be jointly held, this should not be the norm. When talking about your household money, "yours" and "mine" should be replaced by "ours." This is not to condemn the practice of having different budget categories managed by one of the spouses rather than the other. That is just a fact of life—a division of responsibilities. But if you're going to fight over money, start out on the right foot by always speaking of "our money."

Third, if you are the wife and you are responsible for the family's finances, do nothing to take away or hide or relieve the consequences of your husband's profligacy or laziness. Do not remove any slightest responsibility from him by putting the kids in day care so you can work. You take a job and inevitably you will do very well at it, thus playing right into his hands, confirming to him that he is an unappreciated, weak, incapable husband married to an omnicompetent wife, and that he shouldn't feel responsible to provide for his wife and children. After all, that's just an old way of thinking. We're beyond that now.

If you want your husband to be a man, don't become one yourself. Instead, do everything you can to set him up for success. Let him take responsibility and make decisions. Be helpful, and don't whine about all the dumb mistakes he makes. Also, don't cultivate dependence on your parents. And certainly don't agree to his demand that you not honor the Lord with tithes and offerings.

Don't act as if you don't notice his sins related to work and money. Don't save him from them. Put the whole entire weight of your food and home and heat and air conditioning and transportation and medical care and braces for the kids on him and tell him you know he is fully able to bear that weight, because after all, he is a man.

This is not to be dismissive of truly difficult financial conflict in marriage. We recently heard of a heartbreaking situation. We knew a man who lost his job and floundered for several years. He tried a little of this and that in attempts to support his family, but when positions he was qualified for came along, he wasn't hired It was excruciating. After some years in this funk, the husband and wife had used up all their savings and couldn't keep up with their mortgage, so they sold their house and moved into a small rental. They planned to put their home equity into savings to use when they could afford to buy a house again.

One night when the couple was out for dinner, the husband told his wife he had invested their equity in a startup. She broke down and sobbed.

Do not let things get to this point. Being a submissive wife who cultivates a quiet spirit is entirely compatible with taking the needs of your marriage and family—as well as your conflict with your husband—to your elders and pastor for counsel and help. It is central to their calling as officers of the church to help in spiritual difficulties such as this. You and your husband need their care.

We thank God we have the privilege of serving in a church

whose elders and pastors are willing to get their hands dirty as agents of reconciliation between husbands and wives. Look to your elders, pastors, and their wives for help. Then listen to them.

Of course, this brings us back to our first recommendation about money fights, and it's true about fighting in general: Get help. We are part of the body of Christ, and the elders are supposed to shepherd us. Elders should never ignore a situation where a family is crashing and burning. The Apostle Paul had a context and names when he admonished the believers in the church in Thessalonica, "If anyone is not willing to work, then he is not to eat, either" (2 Thess. 3:10).

Sex

Sadly, the sexual union is often fraught with tension and misunderstanding. The marriage bed should be full of loving intimacy, but consider how often it is surrounded by anger, frustration, and fights. We shouldn't be surprised that Satan attacks this beautiful union of the husband and wife which represents the union of Christ and His Bride. Satan hates Jesus Christ and His Church. Thus he hates faithful husbands and wives, and the beauty of the marriage bed.

There are many sources of conflict over sex. Sadly, today, one of the most common is the pain husbands and wives bring into the marriage from sexual sins during childhood. This includes sins they themselves have committed, but also sins which have been committed against them.

Little ones are now exposed to pornography so early in life. Many children are molested and raped, and these things create terrible pain. They may work to shove it down inside of themselves, but it can't be buried and its effects on the marriage bed can't be ignored. Our involvement in sexual sin during childhood colors and corrupts sex in our marriages, often in ways we can't even recognize. If your grandpa touched you in certain ways when you were little, your husband touching you in similar ways is almost certainly going to trigger fear and disgust. However, if you have spent years trying to bury this terrible pain, you may not understand why your husband's touch makes you feel revulsion.

An honest attempt to deal with our childhood abuse is painful and takes hard work for quite a while, but it is important for you and your husband's future happiness. As with money, please get help.

One woman we knew was going deeper and deeper into depression when her husband came to us for help. He was the only person who knew his wife's father had raped her when she was five, and then continued abusing her sexually in other ways for years. Now, forty-five years later, she told us she had intended to take this secret to her grave. But it is not that simple. These memories have a way of catching up with us and wreaking havoc in our lives and marriages. As more and more of these situations have come to light, often in the press, it is tragic how often fifty years have passed before the victim is willing to talk. People suffer years of depression, drug or alcohol abuse, and conflict in marital intimacy, all in order to bury shame.

A young mother who was molested by her brother when she was a little girl called one day to admit that her anger at her husband and children was getting out of control. We encouraged her to get counseling. She needed help peeling away the layers of pain, resentment, and bitterness she was carrying. She had not connected the dots to lay the blame where it belonged. She was not actually angry at her husband and children, but at her parents and the brother who had sinned against her. She needed help working through these difficult issues. She was not alone. If they're doing their jobs, your pastor and his wife have heard many such stories before, and they'll be willing to help.

Another reason there is conflict over sex is based in the differences of the sexes.

God created men and women differently, with different sexual triggers and different needs. The goal is to work together. To communicate together about your needs and desires. We all know men are aroused visually—often very quickly. They are able to get into the sex act quickly, and often they seem to want to get it over with quickly, as well.

Their wives, on the other hand, need more time and have different triggers. They want to be wooed. They want to know their husband cares about them. They will be much more open to sex if he has done the dishes or helped put the kids in bed. They need longer foreplay.

The husband who does not care about this is a foolish man. Similarly, the wife who is not very interested in sex and is always holding out for the perfect scenario is also behaving foolishly. She needs to be willing to have sex more frequently than she might like. She needs to be willing to meet her husband's needs more often than she might desire.

Of course, these are generalizations, but the point is to get to know the needs and desires of your own spouse. Communicate. Try to understand your own needs and be willing to talk about them. Certainly we all know how difficult it can be to talk these things over, but it is work that must be done if we want our intimacy to grow and become more tender and loving.

Don't settle for a marriage union that is unsatisfying. Work at it. It has the potential to get better over time, as your marriage matures through the years. On the other hand, the aging of our bodies can bring new challenges, so deal carefully and patiently with your spouse as desire and responses change over time.

Whenever there is a forum on marriage with a Q & A, the question is asked, "How often should we have sex?" To the women Mary Lee says, "More often than you would like." You have to save some of your energy for your husband, for the bedroom. Try to get to bed earlier. Wear a negligee, take a bath, and light some candles. Such small things can help put you in the mood. On the other hand, be willing to forgo all of this and make love quickly just before you fall asleep. There are times for this too.

A common misconception about sex is that it should be spontaneous. But why? We eat three meals a day, and some of those meals are special, and others not so much. It's the same with sex: it can be like a steak dinner or a quick peanut butter and jelly sandwich. That's fine. We don't grill every night. Sometimes we just want mac and cheese—comfort food.

Yes, you can plan sex. If we don't have on our mental calendar to save time and energy for sex, it will rarely happen. Couples today live at breakneck speed.

The most obvious way to plan your sex is to have a date night. Now I don't even mean you must get a babysitter, take a walk, and go out to dinner. You can plan to spend Friday nights together, putting the little ones to bed a little earlier, having a special dessert (or just popcorn), watching a movie, then going to bed to finish the evening with sex. Many couples do this anyway, but some of them would cringe if it were suggested that they planned their sex. But there's nothing wrong with it. At least it happens.

But to answer the question of how often, twice a week is good. For a healthy marriage, once a week seems necessary—at least to us. But go ahead, have an argument with your spouse about it.

Sadly, even among Christians, it is often true that years of pornography use have left your husband jaded, so he's disinterested in manly sex with his womanly wife. In this case, he needs to repent of his adultery against her, turning back to her by initiating intimacy more often. If she desires sex more often than he does, he must be willing to meet her needs. This is part of the give and take in healthy marriages. Like everything worthwhile in life, work on it.

And never forget the Apostle Paul's command:

> The wife does not have authority over her own body, but the husband does; and likewise also the husband does not have authority over his own body, but the wife does. (1 Cor. 7:4)

Children

Many married couples are quick to describe their firm beliefs and biblical practices concerning childrearing. Usually, they inherited these beliefs and practices from their parents and think what they believe and do is what everyone does (or should do). Maybe the most frequently repeated of such inherited wisdom is, "Never fight in front of your children." If all this means is "Don't scream at your husband or wife in front of your children," or "Don't call your husband stupid in front of your children," we can all agree.

But don't try to hide the fact that there is sometimes conflict between husband and wife. It is helpful to your children to see and hear some disagreements, and then to see the resolution; love lives on. We have one friend who never saw her parents fight, and then the first time she and her husband had a fight she thought they were headed for divorce.

Your children need to know arguments are part of life. It is not the end of the world. To see you hugging and kissing afterwards is reassuring to them. Too often in marriages where the husband and wife pride themselves on never fighting in front of their children, the substitute ends up being hours and days of tension and silence. This is not acceptable.

Whether your conflict is in front of your children or about your children, stinginess in confession and forgiveness are no part of God's plan for marriage. Do not continue to punish your spouse for whatever was said or done. Get over it. Keep short accounts. One of you needs to break the silence and tension. You be the first to confess your sin. Ask God to show you what it is, then take the difficult step of apologizing and asking for forgiveness. What a gift for your children to observe!

One of the reasons children are a source of tension is that the husband and wife come from different traditions and ways of handling things. Add to this that husbands and wives are two different sexes bringing different strengths and weaknesses. Men and women look at things differently and respond differently. Men take initiative, cultivate firmness, and are born to protect. Women are nurturing, tender, and protective—but protective in a different way.

If you need these generalizations to be proved to you, go into the bedroom with your husband, take off your clothes, and see what God has made. As Jesus declared, "He who created them from the beginning made them male and female" (Matt. 19:4).[1] Your body parts make the above things as clear as clear can be, even though the whole world is insane in its efforts to deny them.[2]

But back to God's glorious male and female.

When a son is being bullied by a neighbor boy, the father may tell his son to toughen up and give him permission to punch the kid. Few mothers would approve. Mothers want to protect their son, so they'll try to keep him inside, making sure her boy is not outside at the same time as the bully. Or, say a daughter is being manipulated by an older cousin. The dad might tell his daughter to toughen up and get over it. The mother might accuse him of being insensitive and try to get the girls together to discuss it. It's quite natural for the father and mother to find themselves in conflict over how such situations should be handled.

An area even more fraught with conflict, though, is the discipline of our children. Again, the father and mother come from different backgrounds. The wife may never have been spanked, whereas the husband was raised in a home where his father took him into the bedroom or garage for his spankings. The husband and wife may want to defend the way they were raised. On the other hand, one or the other of them may want to go in the opposite direction, being determined not to make the mistakes their own father or mother made. Whichever way it is, no father and mother making decisions about discipline will see things the same.

This happens in so many ways. The dad might feel that lying is the ultimate sin needing immediate and severe discipline. The mother, on the other hand, might feel that her boys punching each other is the ultimate sin needing immediate long talks together about how Christians are to love each other.

Consider also the frequent battleground of church nurseries. A father might want his toddler in the nursery so the rest of the family can focus on worship. The toddler might not want to go into the nursery, so he pitches a royal fit. The mother might want to mollify the child, smoothing things over by bringing the toddler into church and walking back and forth with him at the back of the sanctuary during worship. Meanwhile, the father is determined that his wife not yield to their little one's preferences, so he sets out to win this contest. He spanks the child in the restroom, then again takes the little one to the nursery door. But of course, barely over the spanking, the child starts in again on his screaming which, in turn, makes the father even more determined. So he takes the boy down the hall to the restroom to spank him a second time. Of course, by now, the father has alienated every woman watching, and he feels it. So the next week, he starts reading of the evils of church nurseries posted by women and men in favor of "family-centered churches." That would resolve the issue, he thinks, so he announces to the family that he's decided nurseries are unbiblical and they're going to change churches. At which point, his wife simply melts down. She and their children have many friends in their present congregation, and even though she does really want to be submissive to her husband, she wonders why she can't just walk the toddler across the back of the sanctuary while the pastor preaches. Isn't that a good compromise?

There are no easy answers to these things, but again, swallow your pride and be willing to get help. We are part of the body of Christ for a reason. We are family. We must be willing to go to each other for help and counsel. If a father tends to be too severe in his discipline of the children, his wife will need to be willing to talk to him about it, and maybe ask his favorite elder or the pastor to meet with them to help. Not right then and there, but later when things have settled down.

In our home, it was common that, when one of the children was fussy, I would discipline them while Mary Lee would be quick to explain why the child was fussy. It was really her fault because she'd taken the kids shopping and they'd missed their naps. It was just before dinner and they were getting hungry. It was bedtime and they were tired. I'd try to explain, that whatever the reasons, the behavior was still not acceptable, and often I'd go ahead and discipline them. Not in anger, but because they needed to learn not to act that way. Mary Lee has since said she had to learn over time to be quiet and let me do my job. And as she watched the behavior of so many of our friends' children as they grew older, she's admitted that she's become thankful for my discipline.

By the way, the first part of the nursery scenario above is identical to a situation we got texts about just yesterday. A young father reached out for counsel. He wanted to know whether or not to keep fighting his toddler over going to the nursery. He believes in spanking and knows we certainly do too, so he was surprised when Mary Lee told him to back off.

Choose your battles and make sure you are winning battles at home before you get all intense at church, home fellowship group, or a picnic with friends. Discipline your children at home so they are pleasant to be with outside your home. Otherwise, you might find that your friends no longer ask you over because your children are so far out of control. If your time together is dominated by children whining, talking over adults, interrupting, crying, and saying they don't like the food your hostess made, you can be sure your hosts won't invite you back.

In our congregation, the nursery has been closed this past year because of Covid. Which means all the children in the congregation have been in worship for this time. One newer young couple has toddlers who were quite disruptive, and the parents seemed clueless. How did we respond? One of our pastors talked to them, explaining how disruptive their children were, and he encouraged them to ask advice of another couple in the congregation with several children who are generally well behaved. They did and all was well.

We could go on and on with scenarios that are frequent causes of fear and conflict for fathers and mothers raising their children, but you know full well what the issues are in your own home. Don't be hesitant to get help. Ask for counsel. Look around at the families in your church, noting which parents are doing a good job, noting which fathers and mothers you respect because they seem to be loved and trusted by their children. Ask them for advice. Ask them for prayer.

Proverbs is all about learning the difference between the wise man and the fool. Frequently, I sum it up to young men this way: The wise man seeks counsel and loves those who instruct and rebuke him, whereas the fool refuses counsel and hates those who try to instruct or rebuke him. Which are you, husband? Which are you, wife?

Before concluding our discussion of conflict, let's read and meditate on just a few verses from Proverbs:

> A wise man will hear and increase in learning,
> And a man of understanding will acquire wise
>   counsel. (1:5)

> The way of a fool is right in his own eyes,
> But a wise man is he who listens to counsel.
>   (12:15)

> Oil and perfume make the heart glad,
> So a man's counsel is sweet to his friend.
>   (27:9)

Now then, let me exhort you one final time to have faith for conflict. God uses it in our marriages. There are times when nothing other than conflict will purify us individually and together. Concerning conflict in the church, the Apostle

Paul writes, "There must also be factions among you, so that those who are approved may become evident among you" (1 Cor. 11:19). Nineteenth-century theologian Charles Hodge comments on this statement:

> It is a great consolation to know that dissensions, whether in the church or in the state, are not fortuitous, but are ordered by the providence of God, and are designed, as storms, for the purpose of purification.[3]

As in civil society and the church, so also in marriage and family life: our conflicts are not desired or welcome, but we should have faith that they are ordered by the providence of God and that these conflicts will purify us.

Chapter 9
Labor of Love

Whatever you do, do your work heartily, as for the Lord rather than for men, knowing that from the Lord you will receive the reward of the inheritance. It is the Lord Christ whom you serve.

— Colossians 3:23-24

Do you love work?

It's true some work is mind-numbing and exhausting while other work is deeply fulfilling. But let me answer for myself: Yes, I love work. And we should love work, but why?

Work is good. Physical work makes us hungry. It leaves us ready to sleep. It makes our sleep deep and satisfying. I could go on, but what we must recognize is that work is a blessing. It's not to be put up with for forty hours a week so we can really live on the weekend.[1] Work is really living—the way God made us to live.

Whether or not you have a good boss or anyone appreciates you, you should be thankful for work, because work is a gift from God. We know this because God established work in the garden of Eden before the Fall, when all was perfect:

> Then God said, "Let Us make mankind in Our image, according to Our likeness; and let them rule over the fish of the

> sea and over the birds of the sky and over the cattle and over all the earth, and over every creeping thing that creeps on the earth." God created man in His own image, in the image of God He created him; male and female He created them. God blessed them; and God said to them, "Be fruitful and multiply, and fill the earth, and subdue it; and rule over the fish of the sea and over the birds of the sky and over every living thing that moves on the earth." . . .
>
> Then the LORD God took the man and put him into the garden of Eden to cultivate it and keep it.
>
> (Gen. 1:26–28; 2:15)

If you have been blessed with children, you know being fruitful and multiplying is work. But here in Genesis, we also read that man is called to rule all living things, to subdue the earth, and to cultivate and tend the garden of Eden. This work is what man was to spend his days doing in the state of perfection, and we will spend eternity working in Heaven.

In Heaven, we'll work at worship, but Isaiah reveals other work God's people will be engaged in then. In the New Jerusalem, we are promised,

> There will no longer be heard in her
> The voice of weeping and the sound of crying.
> . . . .
> They will build houses and inhabit them;
> They will also plant vineyards and eat their fruit.
> They will not build and another inhabit,
> They will not plant and another eat;
> For as the lifetime of a tree, so will be the days of
>   My people,
> And My chosen ones will fully enjoy the work of
>   their hands. (Isa. 65:19, 21–22)[2]

Sadly, like everything else God created, after the Fall things are corrupted. Work is no exception, and this in many ways. God placed the curse of pain on Eve's childbearing and Adam's cultivation of fruit. Work is also often corrupted by the sin of slothfulness. Many of us work half-heartedly or resentfully. Employers refuse to pay a fair wage. Still, let us remember that God is kind and patient so that He might lead us to repentance.[3] Our heavenly Father continues to bless our work, making it profitable.

Early economists were Christians who pointed out that God allowed man to benefit from his labor. God has ordered Creation in such a way that our labor is fruitful, and this for believers and unbelievers alike. As our Lord put it, "Your Father who is in heaven . . . causes His sun to rise on the evil and the good, and sends rain on the righteous and the unrighteous" (Matt. 5:45). Proverbs declares, "In all labor there is profit" (Prov. 14:23).

Work is good. God gave man work to do before the Fall, in the garden of Eden. We will work in Heaven. The Fall corrupted work, yet because of God's common grace, work remains fruitful.

But now, let's turn to labor's fruitfulness and see its dangers. Typically in the Western world, work is rewarded by wages, and usually those wages are money. And money is particularly dangerous. It is a temptation common among men who claim the name of Christ to justify sinful desires by means of pious-sounding phrases. Such men will, for instance, speak of their work as the faithful fulfillment of God's command that we "provide for our own," when their deeper motivation is greed.

In his classic, *A Serious Call to a Devout and Holy Life*, eighteenth-century pastor William Law warns us concerning our motives for work:

> Now to make our labour, or employment, an acceptable service unto God, we must carry it on with the same spirit and temper, that is required in giving of alms, or any work of piety. . . . For if we are worldly or earthly-minded in our employments, if they are carried on with vain desires, and covetous tempers, only to satisfy ourselves, we can no more be said to live to the glory of God, than gluttons and drunkards can be said to eat and drink to the glory of God.[4]

Many believers speak of being their family's "provider," copping a righteous posture as they pile up money and move into bigger houses. They claim their labor is merely fulfilling their desire to be that "good provider." They clothe themselves with the righteousness of being "debt-free" (besides their mortgage, of course), and thus they satisfy themselves that their motivation concerning their work and wages is only godly.

Greed is never far from us. And if we remember our Savior's warnings concerning the deceitfulness of wealth, we will suspect that wealth is fully capable of keeping us deluded while we are clutched in its grip.

Vernon Grounds was the longtime president of Denver's Conservative Baptist Theological Seminary and one of the respected fathers of Evangelicalism. Vern warned against Evangelicals worshiping "the bitch goddess of success,"[5] and if we're honest about our goals and motivations, many of us will admit this danger in our own church, family, marriage, and heart.

President Calvin Coolidge says this about America's character:

> The chief business of the American people is business. They are profoundly concerned with producing, buying, selling, investing and prospering in the world.[6]

Readers might respond, *What's wrong with this? Hasn't God promised His people we will "prosper" in the land He gives them? Isn't Scripture filled with similar promises made by God to His people concerning food and clothing and health and long life and children—everything men have always considered the basics of a prosperous life?*

The truth is, God does not command us to "prosper in the world." He Himself often prospers us, but financial prosperity is not to be any Christian's goal. Serious Christians recognize how dangerous wealth is, remembering the warning of Proverbs:

> Give me neither poverty nor riches;
> Feed me with the food that is my portion,
> That I not be full and deny You and say, "Who is
>   the LORD?"
> Or that I not be in want and steal,
> And profane the name of my God. (Prov. 30:8–9)

When we are "full," we are tempted to deny Jesus Christ. Don't be dismissive of this danger. Take careful note of this warning given the sons of Israel as they were entering the Promised Land:

> Then it shall come about when the LORD your God brings you into the land which He swore to your fathers, Abraham, Isaac and Jacob, to give you, great and splendid cities which you did not build, and houses full of all good things which you did not fill, and hewn cisterns which you did not dig, vineyards and olive trees which you did not plant, and you eat and are satisfied, then watch yourself, that you do not forget the LORD who brought you from the land of Egypt, out of the house of slavery. (Deut. 6:10–12)

In His parable of the soils, Jesus warned us, "The worry of the world and the deceitfulness of wealth choke the word, and it becomes unfruitful" (Matt. 13:22). This phrase "the deceitfulness of wealth" should send a chill down the spine of every man and woman in the Western world today. True, God makes our work profitable, but profitability and prosperity are different things. We should love work, but we must not love money:

> Make sure that your character is free from the love of money, being content with what you have; for He Himself has said, "I will never desert you, nor will I ever forsake you."
> (Heb. 13:5)

If this love of money tempts you, do a search for "money" in Scripture and read all the references. They'll be a good protection. The love of money and greed that is "idolatry"[7] terribly corrupt our work at the point of its motivation. They also deny our Lord. Note that Jesus put it starkly:

> No one can serve two masters; for either he will hate the one and love the other, or he will be devoted to one and despise the other. You cannot serve God and wealth. (Matt. 6:24)

Do not serve wealth. If you do, you *will* despise God.

But aside from greed, there are other sinful motivations that can drive an idolatry of work. Our Lord's instruction is not to judge "according to appearance," but rather "with righteous judgment" (John 7:24) so we need to be careful in diagnosing the true problem here.

You may be wondering at about this point, why all this in a book about marriage? Keep reading.

Many a wife has lamented a husband who is never home

and is a "workaholic," and Mary Lee and I have known and counseled a fair number of couples whose wives suffer something approximating this malady. But is the term workaholic really appropriate? If the man who is an alcoholic loves beer, wine, or booze, the workaholic loves work, right?

Maybe, but maybe not. Sometimes what appears to be workaholism is really family aversion. Work is a tense subject in many marriages, but often not because of greed. In the case of many husbands, it's because they have an aversion to the work of caring for their wives and children spiritually and emotionally. Working at the office day and night six and a half days a week is a good way to avoid these home responsibilities they find so taxing. There are all kinds of work, including the work of husbandry and fatherhood, and working to *provide* for our household often serves as a good cover for not providing for our household emotionally and spiritually.

This is one of the reasons pastors' wives and children are so often bitter about the church their husband and father serves (which is widely recognized as an occupational hazard of the pastorate). Often, it's not really the church that is so demanding of the pastor's time, as much as it is the pastor who uses "ministry" to the congregation as a strategy for avoiding ministering to his own household. When my dad gave me my ordination charge, he warned me:

> Model love and care for your wife and children. Don't sacrifice them and your responsibility for them on the altar of your work and leadership in the church. Determine not to preach to others and see your own children castaways.[8]

At least with the work of builders, painters, and engineers, expressing concern, teaching, and encouraging others are not usually in the job description. But these very things are what pastors spend time doing for their congregation, all the while avoiding doing the same for their families by being out all the time during the evenings and getting home late on Sundays. This makes the pain of a pastor's family aversion much more acute, leading to expressions of frustration by the pastor's wife and children, such as, "You can listen patiently to Mrs. Smith and talk forever to Pastor Michaels and counsel the Murphys week after week, but you never have time to listen to me."

So yes, the kind of work your husband does may have something to do with his failure to love you and your children. It is true that those in the helping professions frequently suffer from emotional exhaustion when they get home, but as Dad warned, we must not sacrifice our family on the altar of our work—any work. Truthfully, the man who never is home in the evenings and on weekends has to look at his reasons carefully, seeing if he truly is absent because of an idolatrous love of work or money, or rather, if work is his perfect justification for avoiding the harder work of loving his wife and children. To examine this carefully, such men need the help of their wife. Even—or especially—when they don't want her help. And again, expect and seek help from the other believers in the congregation, particularly the elders and pastors and their wives, whose responsibility you are.

An ounce of prevention is worth a pound of cure, and Mary Lee and I, along with the other shepherds of our congregation, have often counseled a husband and wife about the dangers of husbands never being home for dinner, never praying for their children as they tuck them into bed at night, never paying attention and expressing affection to their teenage daughter, and never sharing their hopes and fears with their wife. You, too, need a pastor or elder and their wives to help you through these thickets of married life. So have that talk you've been dreading. Ask for help.

We've seen how easy it is for work and its rewards to be corrupted and abused. But we must now reiterate: work is good.

It is not preached and taught enough today that the Fourth Commandment is not just a command to rest on the Sabbath, but also a command to work the other six days of the week:

> Remember the sabbath day, to keep it holy. Six days you shall labor and do all your work, but the seventh day is a sabbath of the LORD your God; in it you shall not do any work. (Exod. 20:8–10)

Here in His Moral Law, God commands us to work six out of seven days each week. Work is simply the fulfillment of God's creation order—what theologians speak of as a "cultural mandate" binding on all men, both wicked and righteous. In the New Testament, we read that God's command to work is to have a penalty that helps us obey it: "If anyone is not willing to work, then he is not to eat, either" (2 Thess. 3:10).

Is this penalty enforced in any of our churches and homes today? Do we have husbands in our congregations who are lazy and don't work? Do we know mothers and wives in our church who are lazy and don't clean or cook? Do we have a pastor who is lazy and doesn't visit, study, or pray? Of course, of course, and of course.

These questions might make you uncomfortable. Perhaps you can't think (or don't want to think) of anyone in your church who is lazy. Would you rather assume this was only a sin in the New Testament church? Maybe this penalty was only to be enforced in the New Testament church? Do you assume this command and its corresponding penalty have no binding authority on Christians and churches today?

On the contrary, the Fourth Commandment's requirement that we are to work six days a week is perpetually binding on all, and this apostolic penalty written to the church in Thessalonica has constant application to our congregations today. Just as we always have the poor among us, we always have the lazy among us, and it is from love for God and compassion for our fellow believer who is lazy that we rebuke and discipline him.

There are places where Scripture is quite specific about our sins, and one of those places is in the Apostle Paul's letter to the Ephesians when he gives instructions concerning the church's discipleship of former thieves:

> He who steals must steal no longer; but rather he must labor, performing with his own hands what is good, so that he will have something to share with one who has need.
>
> (Eph. 4:28)

Manual labor is a good antidote to stealing. Earning wages they can share with others who are poor is a good motivation for former thieves in their newfound honest labor.

That last statement cuts across the grain of many of us, even Christians. It's common for us to think of work as a way to earn money for our needs—and then, when those are satisfied, for our desires. And of course, God *is* kind to us by giving us the fruits of our labor:

> As for every man to whom God has given riches and wealth, He has also empowered him to eat from them and to receive

his reward and rejoice in his labor; this is the gift of God.
(Eccles. 5:19)

But note again what the Apostle Paul told us our prosperity is for: "something to share with one who has need." We work not just for ourselves, but so that we may be generous to others. The neighbor who needs a car for a while to go to work. The widow in the church who needs a new HVAC unit. The Hispanic restaurant owner who's scraping by and would welcome a generous tip from a Christian. It's not enough to not steal and not be lazy. We should be generous. It's a sign of our fruitfulness for the Lord: "Our people must also learn to engage in good deeds to meet pressing needs, so that they will not be unfruitful" (Titus 3:14).

If we have nothing to be generous with, we are being unfruitful. Whether from laziness or stinginess, the effect is the same: we're robbed of the honor and opportunity of participating in this part of God's economy. Let's put it this way: the thief, the lazy man, and the cheapskate are all birds of a feather. They all refuse to honor God by showing generosity with the fruits of their labor. And so, the reason the man who doesn't work must not eat is that any food he eats has been gained by theft.

Some years back, a single young man in our congregation came to the attention of our officers for his failure to follow through on work he'd promised to do for people in the church, mostly tech support (which was child's play for him). He was a sweet and helpful guy everyone liked despite his perpetual failure to deliver. But finally after a number of years, the time of accounting arrived, and the presenting issue was not his help promised to fellow believers, but the paid work by which he supported himself.

One day in a discussion among some of the officers, one

of them said he'd given up talking to this man about the needs of individuals in the church, because he never kept his commitments. He added something few knew, that this brother lived off the wages he earned doing infrequent work programming for a company in another city, and that he'd held this "job" for a number of years. The employer was interested in as much work as this man was willing to do, yet he only worked for them a day or so every week or two because that was all it took to provide enough for himself to live on.

Those listening were scandalized, realizing how lazy this nice, gifted, sweet, single brother actually was. He was liked so much by so many of us, but it dawned on the officers that this man needed discipline. So the elders met and discussed it. After an hour or so, the board of elders decided to send a smaller group of those present to inform this brother than he was sinning by not working—and furthermore, that his failure to work was stealing which must not continue. They were to explain to him that he had the means of earning a good wage, and thus was fully capable of sharing his wages with those who had needs. They were to tell him the board of elders had decided that he needed to take a full-time job, and that whatever job he took, he needed to hold it for at least six months. If he took it and left the position (or was fired) within the first six months, they would proceed to formal discipline.

Does this shock you? Let me admit the whole matter was something of a shock to me. I'd never seen an elders board take such a man in hand before. We'd had such men and women in the congregations I'd served, but never had their sin come before the board of elders, let alone received the elders' censure and the threat of formal discipline. My own opinion is that this brother received this loving rebuke partly because he had proved meek and submissive in his relationships with his elders, so it was the conviction of the board that he would respond well to their rebuke.

Sure enough, he didn't get mad and find another church. He didn't cut off relationships and write a blog post about the elders being on a power trip and abusing their authority. He received the rebuke meekly, and now years later, he is gainfully employed in his field, and carries more than his weight in caring for the needy financially. Join us in praising God for one more case of loving discipline producing the fruit God promises.

Not every lazy person should be addressed this way, but what do your elders and pastors do with laziness in your members? Are there not many spouses and children who would breathe a sigh of relief if their shepherds dealt firmly with family members who refuse to work? It may be a husband who changes jobs every year. It may be a wife who refuses to cook or clean her house or do laundry. It may be a son who is twenty-one and lives in the basement, spending his time watching pornography and playing video games. It may be a man who applies for jobs regularly but won't lower himself to deliver pizzas or clean carpets and bathrooms or greet people at Walmart as he waits for someone to offer him his perfect job.

It doesn't matter whether it's a man or a woman, old or young. If you don't work, you need discipline. It might be hard to keep him from eating in our wealthy, decadent world, but where there's a will, there's a way. Admonish him. Admonish her. Tell them that if they dismiss the elders' admonishment, they may expect formal discipline. That's how serious work is, and if you are the wife of a lazy husband, you will be thankful for this compassion given to your husband by your elders and pastor. Yes, he may leave the church rather than repent, but even that is a matter of praise, that the sin in his life was addressed by faith in a biblical manner. Not everyone who leaves a church under discipline hardens his heart forever. Sometimes discipline produces fruit years later, and for that you must have faith.

Three things before we bring this chapter to an end.

First, it's particularly difficult to know how to deal with a slothful wife. The natural place to turn when a *husband* doesn't work is the elders he's promised to submit to, but the proper place to turn when a wife and mother is lazy is her husband. Her husband is the first person given authority over her by God, which makes things complicated.

When a man doesn't work or keep his house and household in good order, it is appropriate for the elders to deal with him, but when a woman doesn't keep her house and household in good order, it is her husband who is responsible to correct things. Husband, I hope you have older women[9] of the church—usually pastors and elders' wives—who notice and try to help, but even if they don't or won't, you cannot escape your obligation to wife, children, and home. You must recognize this responsibility and deal with things. Don't pretend you are ignorant of your kitchen being a shambles and your laundry room being a junkyard and the children's bedrooms being a foot deep in cast-off clothes, and breakfast, lunch, and dinner never being ready. Take things in hand. This is your duty before God.

Second, let me address fathers and mothers together. You are the ones who should teach your children to work. Don't leave it to their first boss at a fast food restaurant to instruct them in timeliness, order, initiative, and keeping at menial tasks. It is part of childrearing to present your children to the world ready and able to hold down a job and make their boss happy. I'll never forget hearing through my wife that our first child's employer was impressed by our high-school daughter's work ethic. What a joy that was.

When I was a child under my parents, my sister taught me how to clear the table and clean up the kitchen, and this was my job every night, without fail. To this day I take joy in cleaning, whether it's cleaning kitchens, cleaning bathrooms (also my responsibility as a child), washing windows, vacuuming (my brother David's favorite job), weeding, cutting the grass (also my responsibility as a child), or any number of other menial tasks. When I was in high school, I spent a summer cleaning bathrooms in a motel, and that has been so very helpful to discipline my pride to this very day. The man who takes pride in cleaning bathrooms will never lack a job.

Work can be nasty and humbling, and subject to sinful motives. Dignified work we enjoy can be hard to find. Work that uses our gifts in a fulfilling way can be rare. Nevertheless, God commands us to work, and work is a blessing. Build your marriage and household on this biblical truth.

Last, but not least, don't expect God to bless your work and provision for your household if you don't honor Him with your tithes and offerings. Tithes are what we owe the Lord for the maintenance of His church and worship, while offerings are what we present Him from the love and gratitude we feel for His extravagant provision for our every need, both physical and spiritual. We have reflected this distinction in our worship at Trinity Reformed Church by using these words in our Lord's Day worship liturgy: "Now, let us present to the Lord His tithes and our offerings." I'll avoid the debate over whether tithing is something still commanded in the New Testament church. (Yes, it is.)

Mary Lee and I had a lot of difficulty early in our marriage trying to be faithful in tithing to the Lord. We were very poor when we married. In our house, we had an amp, a turntable, about a hundred records, a mattress (on the floor), and a single bureau for Mary Lee's clothes. Nothing else. No table or chairs—when we ate, we sat cross-legged on the floor. No phone, either, so when elders from our church came to visit, they simply showed up, driving all the way from Shorewood Hills on Madison's west side to South Park Street, hoping to catch us at home.

Although my dad was almost always right in his (rare) advice given to us, one time he was wrong. He said to me that, given how poor we were, we might want to consider not giving to the Lord until we had more money. Thankfully, we didn't take his advice. In principle, we were committed to giving to the Lord even while poor—and yet, each Lord's day, we ended up not having anything to put in the offering plate. It was frustrating, and sad. Week after week, we fought about it. It wasn't that one of us wanted to give and the other didn't, but that we were frustrated, and that's what we did when we were frustrated—we argued.

One day we were having the argument out on the sidewalk in front of the grocery store, and it hit us: first fruits. The people of God always gave God their first fruits. They didn't wait to see if the harvest was large enough to provide for the Lord's tithes and offerings, but worshiped Him with the firstborn of their sons and livestock, as well as the first fruits of their soil. These belonged to God:

> You shall not delay the offering from your harvest and your vintage. The firstborn of your sons you shall give to Me. You shall do the same with your oxen and with your sheep.
> (Exod. 22:29–30)[10]

> You shall bring the very first of the first fruits of your soil into the house of the LORD your God.   (Exod. 34:26)

LABOR OF LOVE

From then on, we followed the biblical principle of first fruits. You should too.

As husband and wife, don't worship God with your leftovers. Give Him the first and the best. Right when you get your paycheck, set aside your tithes and offerings for the Lord. Don't wait until the end of the month.

This is the most important truth you can follow in your household concerning your work and money.

Chapter 10

One Flesh

Marriage is to be held in honor among all, and the marriage bed is to be undefiled; for fornicators and adulterers God will judge.

— Hebrews 13:4

If you are married, you are joined to your spouse, and the two of you are one. But of course, that joining is never completely fulfilled. The joining in marriage is both a fact and a command. You *are* joined to your wife or husband, and you *are to be* joined to your wife or husband. The two of you are one, and you are to become one. God has done it, and He commands it.

This is the divine blessing of marriage. So then, husbands, be joined to your wife. Enter her world. Join yourself to her mind, heart, and soul. Both of you, husband and wife, are to make yourselves (or maybe I should say yourself) one.

It may be less common now, but for years couples wanted to light candles during their wedding ceremonies. The bride and groom took two outside candles and together used them to light the third center candle. Sometimes, what came next was the bride and groom placing their individual candles back in the candleholder still lit, leaving three candles burning. As a pastor, I'd always have everyone go through everything in the ceremony during the wedding rehearsal the evening before, so we were able to correct this without much embarrassment. I'd ask something like, "Do the two of you become three or one?"

Puzzled, they'd answer, "One?"

"So then, why are there three candles burning?" I'd ask.

Sometimes they'd get it and say, "Oh, we forgot to blow out our candles." To which I'd respond, "Yup," and it would be over.

Occasionally though, the bride would look at me timidly and ask, "But we don't lose our individuality, do we? We're still both individual persons, right?"

If the bride asked this question, I was in trouble because the conversation we were having was in close proximity to the groomsmen, bridesmaids, ushers, and family members, all of whom were watching me closely. If I showed myself to be an insensitive pastor who ruined rehearsal dinners by making the bride cry, things wouldn't go well the rest of the night. Yes, of course the answer was "No, you don't lose your individuality." Nevertheless, I couldn't just leave it there, because the symbolism required that they leave only one candle burning. If their candle lighting ceremony had any biblical significance, it was that the two become one—not three.

After this happened enough times, it occurred to me the wedding rehearsal may not be the best time to explain the significance of candle lighting—how many candles are left burning and what the relationship between individuality and the two becoming one is. As the years went by, if the couple indicated on their wedding planning forms that they desired a candle lighting during the ceremony, the presiding pastor would talk them through its meaning and significance during premarital counseling sessions, when they were alone. No, the groom and bride don't lose their uniqueness and individuality when they unite in marriage, yet the biblical command is that the man is to be joined to his wife and the two are to become one.

Preaching once, I made the mistake of comparing a long and good marriage with a shoe perfectly worn in from long use. The leather and foot adjusted to each other over the years until it was hand-in-glove, foot-in-shoe. "This is what I love about being married to Mary Lee," I said. "We anticipate each other's thoughts, share each other's jokes, like each other's children (obviously). It's so good to share all of life together and find ourselves sharing more and more as the years go by—just like an old shoe."

The women of the congregation were not pleased and let me know directly after the benediction. "Comparing your wife to an old leather shoe!" Harrumph-harrumph.

But hey, who would ever get rid of her husband's old leather boots? You might get away with tossing a ripped T-shirt or threadbare jeans, but unless you really enjoy stormy waters, you'll think twice about tossing his boots.

At first, leather boots are nasty to wear. They need breaking in. Don't buy your backpacking boots right before the trip, or you'll spend your days in pain with blisters growing, then popping, then each step rubbing them raw. The wise man breaks his boots in little by little, for months prior to the trip. But even at the end of that first trip, although his boots are better, they're not as good as they'll be after the following year's trip—and this year after year. In a decade or two, his feet will have changed and the leather will have continued to adjust to him until the man and his boots are very happy together.

Now I'll grant that women, being beautiful as God made them, quite naturally resent any comparison to old leather boots. But the comparison is not in appearance. It's a comparison of mutual adjustment, fit, compatibility, intimate union, oneness.

Here some women might respond that it's not the ugliness of old leather boots they mind so much as the implication that the husband is the foot and they are the shoe. Am I saying it's the wife who should conform to the husband rather than the husband conforming himself to the wife? *It should be a fifty-fifty proposition, they say. If men and women are equal and the two are to become one, it should be equal amounts of compromise and adjustment coming from both sides, from both the husband and the wife.*

Well yes, the man and woman both share being made in the image and likeness of God, and in that sense they are perfectly equal. But please keep in mind that the woman (Eve) was made from and for the man (Adam). She was made to be his helper, perfectly fit for his needs.

This was God's purpose in creating Eve. Daughters of Eve today should not strive against this perfection of purpose, but instead seek to love and live it out each day of their lives. Woman, the sex, was made by God to fulfill His purpose, and so it is that the woman fits her husband.

It's no indignity for any creature made by his Creator to aim to fulfill God's purpose. What son or daughter of God would ever utter such a thing as to say that living as God made him or her is any slightest indignity?

But yes, of course the husband who is godly adjusts to his wife also. Now then, back to intimacy between husband and wife.

Let's talk about the most obvious form of intimacy: sex.

Think of sex this way: Sex is only the final step of the husband being joined to his wife. Sex is only the physical fulfillment of the deepest commitments and desires already present and working their union in minds, hearts, and souls.

Why only physical intimacy, and why only the final step of being joined?

Because separated from the natural development of oneness in other areas of intimacy, physical intimacy bears false testimony and remains unfulfilling to husband and wife.

To husband? you laugh. *Right. My husband is perfectly happy to demand physical intimacy from me whenever he wants. It doesn't seem to matter what's going on between us personally or emotionally. He just quotes the Scripture that the husband has authority over his wife's body and she is to fulfill her duty to her husband, and that's that. Into the sack I'm supposed to crawl, and service him. It's unfulfilling to me. I feel like a piece of meat, but it's never seemed to bother him.*

What's the Scripture the husband is quoting?

> The husband must fulfill his duty to his wife, and likewise also the wife to her husband. The wife does not have authority over her own body, but the husband does; and likewise also the husband does not have authority over his own body, but the wife does. (1 Cor. 7:3–4)

What God actually commands here is not that a wife service her husband, but that both husband and wife fulfill their duty to one another sexually; and that both husband and wife recognize the authority of their spouse over their own body. Yes, the husband has authority over his wife's body, but the wife has that same authority over her husband's body.

Taken as a whole then, what Scripture actually says is that sex is to be mutual. Both husband and wife have the same duty toward one another and the same authority over one another's bodies. This is quite far from what many hurting wives are being told by their husbands.

Earlier I urged you husbands to join yourself to your wife's mind, heart, and soul. Why didn't I mention her body?

Because we must recognize that physical union is only the natural consummation of prior union in mind, heart, and soul. God has made sex to flow from, and be dependent upon, intimacy and union on every other level of life and personhood. Without that, sex is not much different from animals rutting.

Does this mean sex that doesn't begin in the kitchen or flow from a candlelight dinner is no sex at all, but sin? Sometimes yes and sometimes no.

There are times when the husband gets home from a long deployment or business trip and he's too exhausted to catch his wife up with all the ups and downs he's been through and to listen to the challenges she's had with the kids. So they eat with the kids chattering happily, basking in their dad's return, and after putting the kids to bed, they make love and fall asleep in each other's arms. No talking beforehand in the kitchen, no sharing all about themselves with each other, no candlelight dinner—just the kids talking and then put to bed followed by dad and mom going to bed where they love and sleep. That's not sinful sex.

On the other hand, a woman in our congregation writes:

> Do emotions have any place in physical intimacy in a Christian marriage? If a marriage is seriously lacking in emotional intimacy, how is a godly wife to proceed with physical intimacy? For instance, if a discussion early in the day ends with the wife obviously crying, and the husband says nothing more of it and then wants sex, is the Christian wife to just do her duty? Past teachings I've heard on 1 Corinthians 7:3–5 seem to say yes.
>
> How is a godly wife to guard her heart against bitterness toward her husband and God when it seems that the husband's happiness is all that really matters when it comes to intimacy in marriage?

First, to satisfy wives who resonate with this question, let me say that Scripture does not tell the wife in this situation "to just do her duty." Beyond this, of course, the question above doesn't have an easy answer. To be sure, these frustrations and the questions coming out of them are many married women's frustrations and questions.

As it happens, the first paragraph from the wife's perspective was an anonymous question sent in to the women leading an upcoming women's forum in our congregation. One of the women leading the forum commented that this is "the question asked by every young wife," and she suggested this approach:

> I think maybe this is the wrong question to begin with. Just as you point out that emotional intimacy is for men too, physical intimacy is for women too. In a bad marriage, we think that emotional intimacy is for women and physical intimacy is for men. But perhaps if sex is not enjoyable for the woman, it is because sex is done in a selfish, self-fulfilling way, and she hasn't learned how to participate, or tried to teach him how to pleasure her. Flip it around, and perhaps the same thing is true for the man. Perhaps he doesn't enjoy any attempts at emotional connection because they are made in a selfish, self-seeking way, and he hasn't bothered to teach her what he needs.
>
> I would like to encourage our women to ask this question differently. Because the question itself approaches the issue with a false idea, that sex is for men and love is for women. And that the choice we're faced with is either refusing sex when there are everyday speed bumps in the relationship, or promoting bitterness in a wife.
>
> One more thing we need to drill into everyone's heads when it comes to sex: PRACTICE MAKES PERFECT. Good sex with your husband is a skill that is learned over years

of practice, and you both get better at it with time, and it actually gets better and more fun.

What wise counsel. Go back and read the question and you'll see it's set up in a way that the one answering seems to be limited to two choices: either agree that this wife should not have sex with her husband if she cried earlier in the day and he didn't comfort her, or direct her to service her husband, and then be guilty of fomenting bitterness in the wife against her husband and God.

Of course, those aren't the only options. As the leader pointed out, the question is wrong. There are many things a wife can do that are somewhere between those two evils. She may not have intended to claim she is entirely powerless in the face of her husband and bad teaching on 1 Corinthians 7, but if anyone wants power today, all he has to do is present himself as a victim of abusive authority and the world is ready to declare him a victim and to parade their indignation against the authorities who are to blame for his pain.

We could easily fall into thinking: "Bad husband who cares nothing about his wife's emotions and tears. Bad church that forces wives to service their husband sexually, not expecting any emotional intimacy from him. Poor woman who has such a heartless husband and such insensitive pastors, elders, and older women who (if we believe her) teach and apply Scripture in such a harmful way."

Keep in mind that married men share similar frustrations and parallel questions concerning sex and their wives. For instance:

> If a marriage is seriously lacking in sex, how is a godly husband to proceed with keeping himself pure? For instance, if it's been two weeks since the wife has been willing to be

> intimate and she's dismissive of her husband's desires; if she doesn't want sex most any time and only puts up with her husband touching her when she realizes it's been too long since she last put up with it, is the Christian husband just to masturbate? Past teachings I've heard on Ephesians 5:28 and 1 Peter 3:7 seem to say the husband who loves his wife and lives with her in an understanding way won't ask her for sex when she has a headache or is irritable or tired or has to get up early or is having her period or associates sex with sexual abuse she suffered earlier in life or caught her husband looking at pornography two years ago and is angry about it still.
>
> How is a godly husband to guard his heart against bitterness toward his wife and God when it seems that the wife's happiness is all that really matters when it comes to intimacy in marriage?

And once again, we might point out here that the question is wrong. There are many options here between being a callous caveman and growing bitter. The man who takes initiative and does not enable dismissiveness must also consider how to honor his wife:

> You husbands in the same way, live with your wives in an understanding way, as with someone weaker, since she is a woman; and show her honor as a fellow heir of the grace of life, so that your prayers will not be hindered. (1 Pet. 3:7)

But, to the larger point, why begin a chapter on sex with these discussions of emotional intimacy? Instead, wouldn't it be better just to dive into saying adultery is wrong and give some helpful points on avoiding it? Maybe write some on pornography too? Maybe even say something about the evils of LGBTQism, since that's what people are talking about now in the world and the church?

It's true our world is drowning in sexual sin. But no, we're not going down that road. That would be to avoid the real issue behind all sexual sin. Rather, let's ask ourselves this question: What is the evil of sexual sin, and why does God forbid it?

Some people might respond, "Because sexual sin hurts people."

So then, maybe if we found a way to keep adultery from hurting anyone, it would be all right? If the wife agrees to let her husband have an apartment and woman on the side, or the husband acts like he doesn't notice he's being cuckolded, what's the harm? After all, love is never wrong, right?

As Christians, we know that isn't right. But where do we draw the line, and what is our reasoning? Why does God forbid sexual sin?

God forbids sexual sin because when we commit it, we refuse to love Him and we refuse to love one another. Remember what Jesus teaches us about love and the law of God:

> A lawyer asked Him a question, testing Him, "Teacher, which is the great commandment in the Law?" And He said to him, "'You shall love the Lord your God with all your heart, and with all your soul, and with all your mind.' This is the great and foremost commandment. The second is like it, 'You shall love your neighbor as yourself.' On these two commandments depend the whole Law and the Prophets."
> (Matt. 22:35–40)

It all comes back to love. And what does Jesus say love is, really? Love for God and our neighbor is obeying God's commands. So says the Apostle of Love, John (whom Jesus particularly loved): "For this is the love of God, that we keep His commandments; and His commandments are not burdensome" (1 John 5:3).

In our romantic age, we think love is a sentiment. A feeling. An emotion. If you're looking for love, just follow your passion. But God says no. Love is obedience to His commands. And anticipating our objections, He adds that His commands are "not burdensome."

John Lennon said it right: "All we need is love." Then he was shot, died, and stood facing the Judge of all men. This is a good parable for us to remember as we listen to the world speaking of its "passions" and saying love is never wrong.

God is love, and it's from His love of us that He commands us, "Thou shalt not commit adultery." Does this just mean we're not supposed to have sex with someone else's spouse? Not if we realize that obeying God's commands is really about loving Him and loving others. If the law is ultimately about loving God and loving our neighbor, then this commandment must address much more than just copulation. In fact, there are many ways we can commit adultery. Many ways that we can fail to love and trust God with our marriage, and many ways we can fail to devote ourselves lovingly to our husband or wife.

The Westminster Larger Catechism opens up the many ways we commit adultery. Take a deep breath, because it's thorough in a way that tests the patience of us moderns. Yet it's so helpful:

Q. 138. What are the duties required in the seventh commandment?
   A. The duties required in the seventh commandment are, chastity in body, mind, affections, words, and

behavior; and the preservation of it in ourselves and others; watchfulness over the eyes and all the senses; temperance, keeping of chaste company, modesty in apparel; marriage by those that have not the gift of continency, conjugal love, and cohabitation; diligent labor in our callings; shunning all occasions of uncleanness, and resisting temptations thereunto.

Q. 139. What are the sins forbidden in the seventh commandment?

A. The sins forbidden in the seventh commandment, besides the neglect of the duties required, are, adultery, fornication, rape, incest, sodomy, and all unnatural lusts; all unclean imaginations, thoughts, purposes, and affections; all corrupt or filthy communications, or listening thereunto; wanton looks, impudent or light behavior, immodest apparel; prohibiting of lawful, and dispensing with unlawful marriages; allowing, tolerating, keeping of stews,[1] and resorting to them; entangling vows of single life, undue delay of marriage; having more wives or husbands than one at the same time; unjust divorce, or desertion; idleness, gluttony, drunkenness, unchaste company; lascivious songs, books, pictures, dancings, stage plays; and all other provocations to, or acts of uncleanness, either in ourselves or others.[2]

All the duties mentioned above are to keep us from the sins forbidden by the commandment, and the sins spoken of above are sins against our love of God and our love of our neighbor.

"Watchfulness over the eyes," for instance, is the protection of our chastity and purity. Does any Christian man think God is pleased by his gazing on the curves of some woman who is walking in front of him in the aisle of the grocery store? Does he love God? Does he want to please God, or does he just want to please himself? Does he really want his wife knowing how much he desires his wife's bottom to have curves like the woman they're walking behind? Does he really want to jeopardize his wife and children by giving himself to the adultery of lustful glances, which bears the fruit of pornography, abandonment of his wife, and divorce?

"Immodest apparel" tempts men by presenting them with a view of a woman's cleavage peeking out of her blouse. Does any Christian wife think God is pleased by her showing her flesh? Does she love God? Does she want to please God, or does she just want to please herself? Does she really want her neighbor's husband wishing his wife had breasts like hers? Does she really want her neighbor's children threatened by the abandonment of their father because she aroused his lust in a way that fed his desire for younger flesh? Does she love her neighbor?

I could go on to explain each of the duties and sins above, showing how they are the repudiation of love for God and love for our wife, our children, our neighbor's wife, our neighbor, our neighbor's children, but what's the point? When sexual sin is committed, the very nature of such sins is progressive. It really is a slippery slope, and that slope is deadly. The danger doesn't start with copulation, but lustful looks and immodesty. Scripture makes this clear:

> Can a man take fire in his bosom
> And his clothes not be burned?
> Or can a man walk on hot coals
> And his feet not be scorched?

> So is the one who goes in to his neighbor's wife;
> Whoever touches her will not go unpunished.
> (Prov. 6:27–29)

Jesus gave us similar warnings:

> You have heard that it was said, "You shall not commit adultery"; but I say to you that everyone who looks at a woman with lust for her has already committed adultery with her in her heart. If your right eye makes you stumble, tear it out and throw it from you; for it is better for you to lose one of the parts of your body, than for your whole body to be thrown into hell. (Matt. 5:27–29)

The Westminster Larger Catechism is perfectly in tune with Scripture. It's not simply bedding a woman or man other than your spouse that is unloving, but everything leading up to it.

This brings us to something about the very nature of sexual sin which must be said. There is no such thing as victimless sexual sin. There's no "private" sexual sin that doesn't hurt anyone. This is because God designed sex to be relational, between husband and wife. And that means, when sex is corrupted by sin, it always affects everyone around the sinner, no matter how secret they think their sin is.

The husband looking at pornography may think he's not hurting anyone with his sin, but his wife and children suffer, even before he gets caught. (And that's to say nothing of him supporting the slavery which the pornography industry is built on.) But what about a single man? Is he hurting anyone with his pornography and masturbation? Yes, the single man enslaved to pornography robs the people around him of his strength, service, and encouragement. And he robs the single women around him of a good husband, just so he can satisfy his lusts. Sexual sin always has victims.

This includes sexual sin which is supposedly consensual. Even Christians today have come to believe that consensual sexual sin can be victimless. But this is a lie straight from Hell. It is impossible for a child to give his consent for his older cousin to rape him. It's impossible for a primary school girl to give her consent for her teenaged sister to feel her up. It's impossible for a woman walking in the park to give her consent for a man hiding in the bushes to expose himself to her. In each of these cases there is nothing approximating consent on the part of the victim. There is a victim and there is no consent.

So far we all agree, but let me proceed.

Because the cases above (and other similar cases) involve predatorial behavior on the part of someone with greater power abusing that power to the harm of someone who is vulnerable, we aren't afraid to assign blame to the strong and to absolve their victim of guilt in the matter. This is good and right, but what if the two persons committing sexual sin are equal in power and both pursued each other for satisfying their own lusts? In other words, what if the sexual immorality is agreed upon and sought by both parties—what then?

Say, for instance, there are two Christian women in the same small group whose children are best friends, and one day these two women are working cleaning the church nursery and they begin to cuddle and then kiss? Is it consensual?

Not quite. God has ordered physical intimacy so there is always an initiator and a responder. It's the very nature of our bodies. We can't help but live out male and female in our sexual lives. Homosexual pairings, too, demonstrate this with great clarity, to those with eyes to see.

But for the sake of argument, let's grant this cuddling and

kissing is consensual. Both felt it coming and neither stepped back from the precipice. Both wanted it and both felt the thrills of sin as it was committed. Being consensual, then, was it victimless?

No, never. Sexual sin is wrong because sexual sin is never alone. God looks on and hates it, so there's one offended party whose name is God. Sexual sin is a terrible stain on the holiness and justice of God. This sexual sin is also an assault on Christ's Bride, the Church. How awful to bring such wickedness into the church-house and community.

In the end, sexual sin denies the faithfulness of our Lord to His Bride, the Church, and the faithfulness of His Bride, the Church, to the Lord, her Bridegroom. Hosea was a prophet who was sent to God's people to rebuke them for not loving their God, Yahweh. God sent Hosea to the Sons of Israel when they were drowning in idolatry, which is spiritual adultery.

> When the LORD [Yahweh] first spoke through Hosea, the LORD said to Hosea, "Go, take to yourself a wife of harlotry and have children of harlotry; for the land commits flagrant harlotry, forsaking the LORD." So he went and took Gomer the daughter of Diblaim, and she conceived and bore him a son. (Hosea 1:2–3)

Hosea did as God commanded. He then suffered the agony of his wife's betrayal, which demonstrated before the people of God the horror of their idolatries through which they constantly betrayed the God who loved and had made His covenant with them.

This side of the cross, Jesus has purchased His Bride with His own precious blood, and He demands her faithfulness. Shall we lie about His love? His faithfulness? Shall we make the Bride He is sanctifying filthy? You don't ever want to lie about Christ and His precious Bride.

> Husbands ought also to love their own wives as their own bodies. He who loves his own wife loves himself; for no one ever hated his own flesh, but nourishes and cherishes it, just as Christ also does the church, because we are members of His body. For this reason a man shall leave his father and mother and shall be joined to his wife, and the two shall become one flesh. This mystery is great; but I am speaking with reference to Christ and the church. (Eph. 5:28–32)

Sexual sin betrays our precious Lord as well as our husband or wife and our children. For the sake of our concupiscence[3] and lust, sexual sin sells out everyone we hold dearest—starting with our Savior, Jesus Christ.

Run from your lusts. Run from your tempter, Satan. Run to Jesus for help. Run to your husband for intimacy. Run to your wife for tenderness. "Watch over your heart with all diligence, for from it flow the springs of life" (Prov. 4:23).

Speaking of guarding our hearts, the church of the New Testament on view in the Book of Acts demonstrates the wonderful intimacy of Christian fellowship. Repeatedly this and that house are mentioned, showing the first Christians' sweet fellowship was home-centered. It's nice to have church buildings, but despite the utility of fellowship spaces within the church-house, homes are even nicer for encouraging, confessing our sins, and praying for one another. So by all means, open your home to your brothers and sisters in Christ, and their children. It's hard work, but such hospitality yields much fruit for the kingdom of God.

Why bring this up here?

Because opening our homes or attending a small group

where intimacy is cultivated have their own dangers, and principal among them is sexual sin and adultery. Be on guard. Remember the Apostle Paul's command to Timothy, to treat "the younger women as sisters, in all purity" (1 Tim. 5:1–2).

"In all purity." Do not be naive about the dangers of sexual sin, particularly in the intimacy of the Christian home and Christian fellowship. But also, don't allow this fear to keep you from sharing your life and home with brothers and sisters in Christ. As you testify to your faith by sharing your life and home, guard yourself, your marriage, your children, and all those others you are sharing with.

Watch your eyes. Watch the bedrooms and basement. Be practical in your guardianship, and realize it might be your own wife or husband, or your own children, who are the sinners. If you have a young man in need of a home and you offer him yours for a time, don't allow him to be home alone with your wife. Watch to see if he's a flirt with your wife or daughters. Watch to see if your wife or daughters are flirting with him.

One final thing. If your spouse travels for work, your marriage is particularly vulnerable to adultery. Don't fool yourself. Face the danger. Be forthright with your spouse and discuss your concerns. Tell your husband or wife the protections you need him or her to agree to. Don't blush about it. Don't be intimidated by any angry response. Remember the Scripture we cited earlier:

> The wife does not have authority over her own body, but the husband does; and likewise also the husband does not have authority over his own body, but the wife does. (1 Cor. 7:4)

If you have trouble talking about it together in a reasonable way, ask your pastor to meet with the two of you, raise your concerns with him, and receive his pastoral care. It's eternally important.

Let's conclude with something Martin Luther wrote which does a good job of summing up the thrust of this chapter:

> Let me now say in conclusion that this commandment demands . . . also that everyone love and esteem the spouse given him by God. For where conjugal chastity is to be maintained, man and wife must by all means live together in love and harmony, that one may cherish the other from the heart and with entire fidelity. For that is one of the principal points which enkindle love and desire of chastity, so that, where this is found, chastity will follow as a matter of course without any command. Therefore also St. Paul so diligently exhorts husband and wife to love and honor one another.[4]

Chapter 11

Raising Children

Like arrows in the hand of a warrior,
So are the children of one's youth.
How blessed is the man whose quiver is full of them.

—Psalm 127:4-5

If a man and his wife have been blessed by God with children, what joy! He and his wife have been promoted from man and woman to father and mother, and as their family (by God's grace) continues to grow, their joy continues to increase. But what hard work it is.

In the midst of life together as father, mother, and children, though, we must remember why this work is so very difficult and so often leaves us so very fearful, clinging to God for mercy and wisdom. What does Scripture say?

> Man is born for trouble, as sparks fly upward.
> (Job 5:7)

Man is born for trouble because the Fall has brought sin, suffering, sickness, and death. From the moment of conception, each of our sons and daughters will suffer under their first father Adam's sin. Thus David confessed, "Behold, I was brought forth in iniquity, and in sin my mother conceived me" (Ps. 51:5).

David wasn't speaking of any sin on the part of his mother at the time of his conception, but rather his own personal corruption from the beginning of life caused by man's federal head, Adam. Colonial America's first primer taught the letter *A* to little ones through their memorization of this couplet:

> In Adam's fall,
> We sinned all.

Scripture tells us death and sin are passed down to each of us and our children through Adam.[1] This is the sin in which David was conceived, and this is the sin in which every husband and wife, every father and mother, and every one of our sons and daughters is also conceived.

It is popular today in Christian circles to talk as though children are born without sin, as if they become sinners when they are old enough to commit a sin. Of course those who teach this are very vague as to how old "old enough" is, and what would qualify as a sin. This teaching goes against the plain declarations of Scripture, that from the moment of conception our little one is, at the very depth of his being, a sinner. Thus your work is to call him to repent and believe in the only Savior of sinners, our blessed Lord Jesus. It's not just his mind and body you must form, but especially his soul.

How do we form our sons' and daughters' souls?

Outside Proverbs, only a few Scripture passages directly address the challenging work of raising godly children (although truth be told, all of Scripture gives us direction how to raise our sons and daughters). Addressing the matter more specifically, Moses says:

> These words, which I am commanding you today, shall be on your heart. You shall teach them diligently to your sons and shall talk of them when you sit in your house and when you walk by the way and when you lie down and when you rise up. You shall bind them as a sign on your hand and they shall be as frontals on your forehead. You shall write them on the doorposts of your house and on your gates.
>
> (Deut. 6:6–9)

These words of God through Moses—His laws and commands—are to be written on our hearts and the hearts of our children. We are to teach them to our children *diligently*.

"Preach the Gospel at all times. When necessary use words."[2] People like to say this to remind us that it is important to live out our beliefs, and not just speak them. This is a good reminder, but Scripture's emphasis is actually on the use of words. We are to teach God's words to our children. We can't separate godly fatherhood and motherhood from words.

And, of course, there is only one place where God has given us His very words. This is His special revelation fully and completely contained in the sixty-six books of the Bible. Every single word of Scripture is inspired by God and we are to teach those words to our children constantly, repeatedly, using every opportunity, every minute and occasion, and all of our creative gifts to do so.

Yes, we are to have family devotions, but also we are to repeat the words of Scripture in the car, when we're taking walks, when we're on vacation and when we're at home and during meals and when we go to bed and when we get up. The repetition of God's words in our family life is to be ceaseless.

God's words are to permeate our sermons, our homeschool co-ops, our school curriculum, our small groups, our prayer meetings, our college and university educations, our seminary classrooms, our walls, our tweets and posts on Instagram, our music, our prayers. And this doesn't mean that we are to mindlessly repeat portions of Scripture chosen haphazardly. We should choose the verse and passage carefully, some specifically applied to this son and another for that daughter. When we argue, we are to seek to prove our points with the only infallible rule of faith and practice—the Bible.

In my book on fatherhood,[3] I told how my dad quoted Scripture in our home. His quotes were both general (for all the children) and specific (for an individual son or daughter). One of the most frequent Scriptures he spoke to all of us was, "The heart is deceitful above all things, and desperately wicked: who can know it?" (Jer. 17:9, KJV). One verse he frequently spoke to *me* was, "A double minded man is unstable in all his ways" (James 1:8, KJV). Believe me, I needed to hear it. Have faith to speak Scripture to your children.

And speaking of Scripture, here's another passage that directs our care for our children:

> And they were bringing children to Him so that He might touch them; but the disciples rebuked them. But when Jesus saw this, He was indignant and said to them, "Permit the children to come to Me; do not hinder them; for the kingdom of God belongs to such as these. Truly I say to you, whoever does not receive the kingdom of God like a child will not enter it at all." And He took them in His arms and began blessing them, laying His hands on them.
>
> (Mark 10:13–16)

The disciples thought children were a bother, so they rebuked moms and dads for trying to get Jesus to touch their precious

11 RAISING CHILDREN

little ones. Jesus responded by rebuking His disciples for rebuking the moms and dads.

Two stories.

First, a pastor I used to work with came over to our house and sat talking with me at our kitchen island. Excited that a visitor was there, our young daughter came up with her offering for the occasion—a picture she'd just drawn. She was three or so and stood there, lifting her picture up to my friend with outstretched arm and hand, but my friend didn't notice her.

My wife was across the kitchen at the counter, working. She had been watching what was happening and finally interrupted long enough to say to my friend, "She is trying to give you a gift."

He responded by looking down for an instant and taking the picture, but without any verbal acknowledgment or thanks to the little one. As he took the picture, he kept talking to me. It was quite sad. I knew how unimpressed my wife was, seeing how disinterested he was in children.

Second, a story about Mother Teresa. Some years back I was walking across downtown St. Louis with her to the convention center where we had engaged her to speak to the general assembly of our denomination. Mother Teresa was there to rebuke the assembly for their approval of abortion, which she did—and wonderfully so—by saying things like, "If I had the power, I would build a prison and put in it all the doctors who do abortions. They are murderers!"

The whole world knew of Mother Teresa and her work of compassion over in Calcutta (as it was then called). As a nun, she was more famous than her Pope. As we crossed the intersection next to the convention center, we were mobbed by women—mothers and grandmothers pushing through the crowd with their hands extended holding pictures of their children and grandchildren. All they wanted was for Mother Teresa to touch the pictures, thereby giving a blessing. Somehow. Please.

I'd never experienced anything like it. My pastor friend had no time or attention to give my young daughter, but Mother Teresa was doing her best to care for the ewes and their lambs. It was so tender of her.

Now then, back to Jesus. His disciples were just like my friend, the pastor. They thought Jesus' time and energy were too important to be wasted on children, but that wasn't how Jesus saw it, and this dismissiveness toward the children by His disciples angered Him.

If Jesus, a single man in His thirties, made time for the children, how much more should we as mothers and fathers? He has blessed us with sons and daughters who are the fruit of our lovemaking, so how much time and attention do we give them? Do we think of them as an interruption to our real work, or rather do we see our work as an interruption to our children? Of course I'm forcing a false antithesis here, but think about it. Do you consider your children a nuisance and wait for them to go to bed? Are you relieved when you have to go on a business trip? Husband, are you glad your wife is the one who cares for them throughout the day?

Change your way of thinking. Children aren't a bother or a nuisance, but a blessing. They are a blessing from the Lord, and happy is the man whose quiver is full of them. Believe it. Live it. Have faith for this truth.

This is an important lesson. Don't neglect your children. Don't think your business or deer hunting or parishioners or sewing and cooking and gardening and Instagram are more important than your little ones holding out to you a picture they drew for you—or your teenage daughter who wants to tell you everything that happened at school earlier in the day.

11 RAISING CHILDREN

I often talk about my dear friend Rita Cuffey who was a mother to our congregation right up to her death at a ripe old age. Rita had been pursuing a doctorate in astronomy at Harvard until she married one of her fellow grad students, Jimmy Cuffey. When he'd completed his degree, he was hired on as a professor at Indiana University.

Rita and I met weekly while she was alive, and one day she got to talking about how dismissive other faculty wives had been towards her. Without bitterness, she explained:

> When I first moved here, the faculty wives invited me to join their weekly coffee klatch. So I went, but when I got home the children had already arrived home from school, and I'd missed it. When children get home from school, they're ready to talk—to tell their mother everything—and if you're not there to listen, you've lost it all. So I never returned to the faculty wives' coffee klatches. When your children are ready to talk, you have to be there!

Now yes, I can hear the arguments and complaints about Rita's statement: *We have to have two incomes, so I have to work... Don't try to guilt-trip me over not being home when my children get home from school... Not all kids want to talk to their mother... It's not good to let kids blab on and on to their mother as if they're the only person in the world that matters... Kids are selfish and should not be able to waste their mother's time...*

Yeah, yeah, and yeah. But I anticipated these and many other objections to Rita's statement when I wrote it just now, and yet there her wisdom remains, giving off its motherly fragrance. Readers need to think about how we show our disinterest in these little ones God has blessed us with. How unwilling we are to listen to them. What a nuisance it is to stop and patiently let them help us when we're cooking or changing the oil. Yes, of course it's more efficient to do things ourselves, and yet . . .

Jesus didn't stop doing important things in order to give attention to the little babies and children. The important thing was paying attention to them.

And what sort of attention did Jesus give? This too is noteworthy. "He took them in His arms and began blessing them, laying His hands on them."

Touch is so important, and we must stop here to think on it a bit. If you're worried about sexual abuse, one of the best ways to protect your children from this terrible sin is to teach them good touch. It's like learning to recognize counterfeit currency: the best method of training cashiers to spot counterfeit currency is to get them to examine and feel genuine currency. Same with touch. Children familiar with genuine affection and touch will more readily recognize the manipulation, looks, and pettings of the predator.

Scripture is filled with affection and love, as well as the resultant touch that expresses these things we so desperately need for our emotional and spiritual health. Go into any nursing home with your children by your side and watch the men and women there in their wheelchairs or behind their walkers reach out to stroke the hair of your daughter or touch the cheek of your infant or motion to your son to come sit on the side of their bed.

This is beautiful. God made us physical beings. Physical tenderness is no sign of weakness, nor is it lust—let alone lechery. Often I explain to a wife that her husband needs her tenderness, physically, and that he'd be greatly encouraged if she'd tussle his hair, give him a kiss when he gets home, and lean against his shoulder, snuggling up to him on the couch. Then I add that I'm not speaking about sex.

11 RAISING CHILDREN

Most touch between us has nothing to do with lust or sex, and it's a sad day when our sexually debauched culture intimidates us into neglecting non-sexual physical intimacy with those we love—particularly our children. Sadly, the problem is often aggravated by past sexual sin in the lives of fathers and mothers.

Mother, if you were molested as a child, you may think the way to protect your children from such pain and suffering is to have no one but yourself and the nurse or doctor touch them. Wrong. The way to protect your teenage daughter from the boy in the youth group who wants to feel her up is to have your husband hug her and tell her how beautiful she is. All the time. The young woman in the springtime of her life won't need some smooth-faced boy's approval of her body if she has her father's approval of her hair and face and body.

Her body? you may ask in horror. Of course her body. The woman's body is made beautiful by God, and her father is able to tell her so without there being any mistake about his intentions.[4] What a relief to hear you are gorgeous from your father right as you enter adolescence and feel so awkward and ugly. Your dad says, "No, you're beautiful."

One of the most common mistakes Christian parents make today is jealously guarding their children, seeking to keep them close and (as they see it) safe from the contagion of other homes and families—and this even in the church of Jesus Christ. Much of this natural tendency toward jealousy over our children has been intensified by the sexual perversion of our culture as well as the pervasiveness of sexual abuse in the church. It is true there is a world of danger to our children inside and outside the church, but we must not allow the prevalence of sexual sin to rob us of the wonderful and godly influence of brothers and sisters in Christ whom God Himself has placed in our lives for our own well-being, as well as the growth and maturity of our sons and daughters.

I know this is scary to read, but sin is in the world, and that sin is in ourselves and our own homes. And this is the case, not because we've let a pervert into our home, but because we ourselves, as well as our sons and daughters and husband and wife, are sinners. Fact is, we all need the blood of Jesus to wash away our sins, and this isn't true of other believers' homes and families without being true of our own home and family.

It's true there are terrible dangers we must be on guard against. We must teach our children what abuse is; which body parts are private and must never be touched or seen by anyone other than their mommy or daddy. We must teach them that if anyone tries, they are to scream and keep screaming no matter what threat she or he makes to silence them. We are to explain to our young children that they should always come to us and tell us anything that's bothering them. That they can tell us their sins they've hidden and we'll understand and help them with them. That they can tell us their sins because they know we sin too, and because they have seen and heard us ask their mommy, brother, and sister to forgive us.

Then we explain to them that we love them even though they sin like we do, and what's unbelievable is that God is perfectly holy and He loves sinners too. We then give this very concrete warning:

> But sweetie, there may be some time when someone who is a child or an adult, a man or a woman, a boy or a girl, maybe a friend or even one of your aunts or uncles or cousins; someone from church or a teacher or a neighbor boy or girl (or a babysitter) will try to do something to you that's

very wrong. If that ever, ever happens, you scream bloody murder and run.

And one other thing: if anyone at all ever tells you not to tell your mommy or me something, that is the very thing you must tell me or mommy right away, as soon as you can. No matter what they say to scare you. Don't be afraid. I will protect you. Scream at the top of your lungs. Scream and run from them. Then tell us right away. Don't be afraid of them. Whatever anyone tells you not to tell us is the one thing you must *always* tell us.

We live in the midst of danger, but we must not succumb to it in this matter of love and physical intimacy with our children. Daddy's kisses and hugs are our children's protection.

Yes, touch can be perverted, but why allow the abuse of a thing to rob us of the good and right uses for which God created it? Why allow some ridiculous misunderstanding of manliness or safety to keep a father from expressing affection, or hugging, kissing, and wrestling with his children? We could turn the saying around and say the good use of a thing inoculates us against its abuse.

Again, Scripture is filled with records of precious touches, as well as commands to us to reproduce them today. For instance, here's the great recognition scene between Joseph and his young brother, Benjamin:

> Then he fell on his brother Benjamin's neck and wept, and Benjamin wept on his neck. (Gen. 45:14)

There's the tender reunion down in Egypt between Joseph and his aged father:

> Joseph prepared his chariot and went up to Goshen to meet

his father Israel; as soon as he appeared before him, he fell on his neck and wept on his neck a long time. (Gen. 46:29)

There's the deep love of Jonathan and David for one another:

When the lad was gone, David rose from the south side and fell on his face to the ground, and bowed three times. And they kissed each other and wept together, but David wept the more. (1 Sam. 20:41)

Also, we have the terrible sadness of the Apostle Paul's departure from the Ephesian elders:

And they began to weep aloud and embraced Paul, and repeatedly kissed him, grieving especially over the word which he had spoken, that they would not see his face again. (Acts 20:37-38)

Add to this the apostolic commands to Christians to "greet one another with a holy kiss,"[5] and the beauty of physical, non-sexual expressions of tender love is entirely established. And if in the church, how much more in the home?

There's nothing pious about being a prude. There's nothing holy about being a cold fish. "Love one another, even as I have loved you," commands Jesus (John 13:34). Note the physical intimacy described between Jesus and His disciple John during their last supper in the upper room:

There was reclining on Jesus' bosom one of His disciples, whom Jesus loved. So Simon Peter gestured to him, and said to him, "Tell us who it is of whom He is speaking." He, leaning back thus on Jesus' bosom, said to Him, "Lord, who is it?" (John 13:23-25)

Create a Christian home that is perfectly safe, sexually. Touch your children.

Dad was preaching during a chapel service at Wheaton College and, in passing, mentioned that he thought college students would love to get a hug and kiss from their dads. To his surprise, the students stood and gave a standing ovation. That says a lot about the lovelessness of Christian homes, doesn't it?

Now a few words about discipline.

Here's a generalization about men and women. Men are more willing to discipline children than women are. Yes, some women are superior disciplinarians to their husbands, but generally speaking, it's the husband's inclination to spank and the wife's to act as if she doesn't hear the disrespect or see the disobedience.

Two decades ago, I read the most popular Christian book on childrearing. It was very good and our church had the author come out and lead a weekend conference on childrearing, but it was shocking that in his books and talks to fathers and mothers, he completely avoided the subject of marital conflict over discipline of children. Spending much time across years counseling couples having difficulties, Mary Lee and I knew how much marital conflict stemmed from disagreements over the discipline of children, yet he never mentioned it. How could this be? Was he unaware? Had he and his wife always had perfect agreement over the discipline of their own children?

Of course not. He and his wife had fought, and even if they hadn't, he was a pastor and knew full well how many marital conflicts in his congregation had their origin in this tense area. I never brought it up with him because I didn't want to discourage our invited guest who was so helpful in so many other areas. But why do you think he never mentioned it?

It's messy, isn't it? Really, really messy. Addressing it would require addressing authority and submission, wouldn't it? And what traveling speaker, Christian or otherwise, thinks he'll get more speaking engagements by calling husbands to lead in a godly way, and wives to submit in a godly way?

My own father and mother certainly did fight over this, especially their discipline of me. One time my mother went upstairs and had a long talk with Dad while I waited in the living room. In their marriage, Mud was the disciplinarian and Dad was the softie, so readers will understand what had happened upstairs when Mud came back down and said to me, "I should cry more often with your father." I had been the source of their conflict, and Mud was pleading with Dad to take me in hand.

We love our children. And what is more important to us in every fiber of our being than their welfare? And what is more crucial for their welfare than our work raising them in the nurture and admonition of the Lord? If we have conflict over anything, shouldn't we have conflict over this? Aren't our children worth it? Of course we fight over the instruction and discipline of our sons and daughters. There's nothing that matters more to us.

Do you think you can get childrearing right without fighting over it?

If so, you're wrong. You can't. Improvement requires father and mother to criticize and argue with one another. Or, if you prefer this word, improvement requires "disagreement." The exchange of views. To engage in dynamic discourse that yields a better approach than either of you would have come up with on your own is what marriage, fatherhood, and motherhood are all about. Go ahead, have your disagreements.

11 RAISING CHILDREN

Disagreements between father and mother are the rich, black soil children grow best in.

It's reported that a frequent cause of divorce in second marriages is the discipline of children. Who doubts that second marriages bring greater tensions to an area of marriage that—even in the best of circumstances—is a minefield? It would be natural for a mother to be protective of her own children, not trusting their new stepdad's discipline. She might spoil her own children and be punitive toward her husband's children, and this might well drive her husband crazy. On the other hand, he might prefer his own children and show it by making clear they are his favorites.

If you are in a second marriage and struggling with these issues, as I have said over and over again, you need to ask for counsel. Ask a pastor or elder to sit down with you and talk about the tension and ways to resolve it.

One final word to parents: You know how weak and sinful you both are, so claim God's covenant promises for your work with your children. When one of you grows weary and fearful, repeat those promises to one another.

First, God's covenant promise to our father Abraham:

> I will establish My covenant between Me and you and your descendants after you throughout their generations for an everlasting covenant, to be God to you and to your descendants after you. (Gen. 17:7)

Next, God's covenant with the sons of Israel:

> So you shall keep His statutes and His commandments which I am giving you today, that it may go well with you and with your children after you, and that you may live long

> on the land which the LORD your God is giving you for all time. (Deut. 4:40)

God's promise through the Apostle Peter on the day of Pentecost:

> "For the promise is for you and your children and for all who are far off, as many as the Lord our God will call to Himself." And with many other words he solemnly testified and kept on exhorting them, saying, "Be saved from this perverse generation!" (Acts 2:39–40)

God's promise to the Philippian jailer:

> Believe in the Lord Jesus, and you will be saved, you and your household. (Acts 16:31)

Beyond these promises, our heavenly Father also tells us He will stand with us, helping us with the raising of our children:

> All your sons will be taught of the LORD;
> And the well-being of your sons will be great.
> (Isa. 54:13)

> Train up a child in the way he should go,
> Even when he is old he will not depart from it.
> (Prov. 22:6)

We must beware, though, because there are times when, despite God's promises to gather our children to Himself, we resist Him. Then His promise is that He will leave our house desolate:

11 RAISING CHILDREN

> Jerusalem, Jerusalem, who kills the prophets and stones those who are sent to her! How often I wanted to gather your children together, the way a hen gathers her chicks under her wings, and you were unwilling. Behold, your house is being left to you desolate! (Matt. 23:37–38)

Again, is there anything more precious to us than the fruit of the womb of our beloved wife, and the eternal salvation of our children?

So then, do your work. Discipline them diligently. Love them tenderly. Raise them in the nurture and admonition of the Lord. Touch them with love and affection. Pray for and with them. Discuss with your wife or husband how best to respond to this or that child's sin. Protect your children from the wicked, even in your school and congregation and family. Plead with God to help you, reminding Him of His many covenant promises to be a God to you and your descendants after you.

May God give you everything you lack, covering over your sins and mistakes so that you, one day, may have the great joy of seeing your children walking by faith into the kingdom of God.

As I write, I feel the building emotional pressure of those readers who are married couples who are childless and likely working hard not to be resentful over how central children are to what is written here and elsewhere in this book. If that's you, let me commend you. Many of you are reading this chapter despite your anticipation that it would be painful, and that's a mark of spiritual maturity. It's hard to describe the pain of God closing the womb—the anguish of all the tests and drugs and foster children taken into the home in hope of finally being able to adopt a precious little one of their own.

The truth is, you actually can have lots of children, although they may not be children God presents to you as the fruit of your own womb. Nevertheless, you can help the mothers and fathers all around you care for their children. All the children of your brothers and sisters in Christ are children of the church also. God has placed each child out on loan to this or that couple, but as my father said after losing three of His own, God can call in His loan anytime He chooses.

God doesn't just give children to their blood relations—He also gives them to His Bride, the Church. So, in truth, the sons and daughters of the church belong to you regardless of whether or not you gave birth to this little girl or that teenage boy. Care for them. Love them. Protect them from their sin. Guard them from abuse. Instruct them. Admonish them. Stop fixating on, and mourning over, these children not belonging to you. Be a second mother or father, an aunt or uncle, to them. With all purity.

We're not talking about making your church into a commune and the church's nursery into the commune's nursery. We're not a kibbutz in Israel. We're not a missionary boarding school. We're not socialists or communists or Black Lives Matter founders trying to destroy the bonds of marriage and family.

Yet do you remember the promise you made the last time a little one was baptized or dedicated in your worship service Sunday morning? If your church is typical, you answered questions similar to what we ask of the members of our congregation each time one of our little ones is baptized or dedicated:

> PASTOR: Do you, the congregation of this church,
> promise to tell this child of the Gospel of our Lord,

RAISING CHILDREN

to help him learn all of Christ's commandments, and to assist him in living a godly and Christian life in the household of God?

CONGREGATION: We do.

PASTOR: Do you promise to help these parents raise this child in the nurture and admonition of the Lord, so that in due time he may confess faith in our Lord and Savior, Jesus Christ?

CONGREGATION: We do.

Chapter 12

She Is Your Companion

The LORD has been a witness between you
and the wife of your youth, against whom you
have dealt treacherously, though she is your
companion and your wife by covenant.

— Malachi 2:14

Christians go to Scripture to find examples to follow, and there's one example of a godly marriage we might easily miss.

The Apostle Paul left Athens for Corinth, and there in Corinth he set up shop with a Jewish man named Aquila and his wife, Priscilla. Concerning the friendship that developed between the Apostle Paul and this man and his wife, Scripture says, "Because [Paul] was of the same trade, he stayed with them and they were working, for by trade they were tent-makers" (Acts 18:3). The account continues:

> Now a Jew named Apollos, an Alexandrian by birth, an eloquent man, came to Ephesus; and he was mighty in the Scriptures. This man had been instructed in the way of the Lord; and being fervent in spirit, he was speaking and teaching accurately the things concerning Jesus, being acquainted only with the baptism of John; and he began to

speak out boldly in the synagogue. But when Priscilla and Aquila heard him, they took him aside and explained to him the way of God more accurately. (Acts 18:24–26)

This man Apollos was quite the leader, wasn't he? "Eloquent" and "mighty in the Scriptures," he was "fervent in spirit" and preached "boldly in the synagogue."

For these reasons, note carefully what Scripture does *not* say here. Luke does not record for us that Aquila took Apollos aside and corrected him privately, man to man. Rather, it was both Priscilla and Aquila who "took him aside and explained to him the way of God more accurately."

This was doctrinal correction given by a wife and husband, together, to an eloquent and bold man who was mighty in the Scriptures. To make the point crystal clear, Priscilla was not serving the men tea. But lest we jump to the feminists' conclusion that Priscilla was there to demonstrate her superior gifts, seize her moment, and destroy all those patriarchal fetters she and her strong, wise sisters suffered under because of the insecurity of men of the time, note carefully this helpful explanation the Reformer John Calvin gave five centuries ago:

> This was no small modesty which was in Apollos, in that he doth suffer himself to be taught and instructed not only by an handy craftsman, but also by a woman. . . . We see that one of the chief teachers of the Church was instructed by a woman. Notwithstanding, we must remember that Priscilla did execute this function of teaching at home in her own house, that she might not overthrow the order prescribed by God and nature.[1]

Earlier in the chapter, Aquila's name comes before his wife's, but here in the record of their correction of Apollos, the order of their names is flipped: "Priscilla and Aquila." Why?

Bible commentators from both present and past centuries think this change in the order indicates something special about Priscilla's gifts and knowledge.[2] This married couple were a cornerstone of the New Testament church, and a blessing to Paul:

> Greet Prisca and Aquila, my fellow workers in Christ Jesus, who for my life risked their own necks, to whom not only do I give thanks, but also all the churches of the Gentiles; also greet the church that is in their house. (Rom. 16:3–5)

The first thing we actually notice is that Priscilla (referred to here in the diminutive, *Prisca*) and Aquila apparently worked together. They were tentmakers. It is no small feat to work side by side as a married couple. Mary Lee and I know because we used to do it, painting and cleaning houses together. And let's just say it was not our greatest time of togetherness.

Next, both of them (not just Aquila) were dear friends of Paul. We do not know the details, but they risked their lives for him. They were active together in the ministry. Paul refers to them as "fellow workers in Christ." They also hosted a church in their home. This was quite the couple.

Maybe we don't know Scripture and the doctrine of salvation as well as Priscilla and Aquila did, but even if we had knowledge and wisdom equal to theirs, which of our marriages would have the sort of loving intimacy to work so naturally together, taking a man as gifted as Apollos aside and speaking to him helpfully so he was able to serve the church better? Would our marriages be described as being this sort of blessing to God's people? Would your wife and you be able to bear such good fruit together?

12 SHE IS YOUR COMPANION

Barb and Kent Hughes are a couple who were a blessing to Mary Lee and me many years ago, and still are today. Soon after moving to begin ministry in a yoked parish of two churches in the dairy land of Wisconsin, we received the most recent issue of *Leadership* in our mailbox. A magazine for "ministry professionals," it had an interview with several famous pastors' wives, one of whom was Barb. Her husband, Kent, was then pastor of our home church in Wheaton, Illinois. At the time, we didn't know Barb and Kent personally, but we knew they were quite close to my parents, so we were interested.

The interview shocked us. There was a stark contrast between Barb's responses and the responses of the other women. When these other women (maybe five of them) were asked questions relating to their interface with their husband's ministry, they distanced themselves from him, saying their husband's calling wasn't their calling, their husband's work wasn't their work, their husband's needs weren't their responsibility, and on it went.

But not Barb. There shining gloriously amidst these liberated women was sweet, sharp-as-a-tack Barb testifying that she was Kent's wife, that his calling was her calling, his ministry was her ministry, his work was her work, his needs were her responsibility (which gave her joy), and on it went. Repeatedly, Barb confessed her contentment and happiness in being Kent's helper. She was unflinching and irrepressibly biblical. In contrast to her fellow interviewees surrounding her in the room, Barb was *feminine*. In our modern day, could such a woman still exist?

We were so thankful for Barb's testimony that we wrote her a letter telling her of our joy and gratitude for her witness. A short time later, Barb called Mary Lee and asked if she and Kent could come up for a visit. We gladly accepted.

So Barb and Kent drove the two and a half hours up from Wheaton and spent the day with us. You can imagine what a gift this was. We were young, so to have an older pastor and his wife spend a day sharing their wisdom and commitments and showing us their affection was so helpful.

Maybe you feel it's a non sequitur to follow the example of Priscilla with the example of Barb, but they're not as different as they may at first appear. Both women shared in their husband's ministry. Both were helpmates, not seeing themselves as too good or important to help their husbands. Certainly, at their dinner table Barb helped teach many men, and, knowing Barb, we can promise she sometimes took the lead. No doubt Priscilla showed wifely feminine deference to Aquila even as she helped instruct Apollos. And yes, she probably also served tea or coffee or whatever.

Luke held Priscilla and Aquila up as an exemplary couple, and here, Mary Lee and I hold Barb and Kent up as an exemplary couple.

My point is not to talk about pastors' marriages, though, but marriages in general. It could be your pastor and his wife. It could be an elder or a deacon and his wife. It could be your small group leader and his wife. It could be a missionary and his wife. It could be your son and his wife. It could be your dad and his wife—your mother. It could be you and your wife, and that's what we're really concerned with now.

We all need such gifts from married couples—especially the gift of seeing them work seamlessly together. The growth of our sons and daughters physically, emotionally, and doctrinally also depends upon watching such a seamless working relationship between their father and mother.

If the wife is unwilling to grow in her wisdom and knowledge, or the husband is unwilling to defer to his wife in areas where she is superior to him in wisdom and knowledge, it all goes to pieces. Then, what Apollos or your pastor or your sons and daughters will remember is that togetherness is not one of the strengths of your marriage.

Is this what you want? When you're together with others, do you want them feeling awkward about the two of you because your wife is filled with herself and overpowers her husband or corrects him at every turn—or your husband is insecure and, when your superior knowledge and wisdom might cause you to be the one who shines in the presence of others, he shuts you down?

How do we cultivate a marriage like the marriage of Aquila and Priscilla that blesses others? How do we work toward a marriage that is capable of natural relations with others in the church who are pleased to spend time with us and listen to our counsel? The answer is to grow together in intimacy, not just sexually, but emotionally, intellectually, and doctrinally. To become true companions.

Companionship. That's an important word. Let's focus on it for a moment.

Historically, Christians have confessed that Scripture gives three purposes of marriage. The seventeenth-century outline of Scripture's truths called the Westminster Confession of Faith lists them:

> Marriage was ordained for the mutual help of husband and wife; for the increase of mankind with a legitimate issue, and of the Church with an holy seed; and for preventing of uncleanness.[3]

These three purposes—companionship, children, and the prevention of sexual sin—are repeated across church history, most notably by pastors at the beginning of wedding ceremonies. Listen for them. Here's the liturgy we use in our church:

> The union of husband and wife in heart, body, and mind is intended by God: First, for the procreation of children, to be brought up in the fear and nurture of the Lord, and to the praise of His holy name. Second, it was ordained for a remedy against sin, and to avoid fornication; that such persons as have not the gift of continency might marry, and keep themselves undefiled members of Christ's body. Third, it was ordained for the mutual society, help, and comfort that the one ought to have of the other, both in prosperity and adversity.

"For the mutual society, help and comfort that the one ought to have of the other." This is companionship. God saw it was "not good for the man to be alone," so He created woman. Adam needed a companion, and God gave him one (Gen. 2:18–25).

Today, man needs companionship just as much as Adam did. If you are married, you are to cultivate this companionship together, husband and wife.

Companionship can take many forms, and it changes through the years and seasons of life. Some couples are newly married, others are facing the challenges of young children God has blessed them with. Another season arrives, and couples face the departure of their first child from their home, then the empty-nest time of life. This is followed by the final years. Throughout these seasons, those who do the necessary work cultivating it enjoy companionship's many blessings.

Companionship doesn't come as easily as we may think. Like all of life's blessings, companionship yields its joys most to those who work at it. So work at it. Work to follow the godly example of Priscilla and Aquila.

How do we work at it?

For starters, companionship requires that we share each

other's thoughts. And if we want our companionship to be godly, we will work to make God's thoughts our thoughts, together. Jesus promised, "If you continue in My word, then you are truly disciples of Mine; and you will know the truth, and the truth will make you free" (John 8:31–32). Our minds are renewed as we grow in God's truth. Growth in His truth frees us from the terrible pressures in our culture to click "Like" on the social justice warriors' stupidities incessantly repeated by relatives and friends on social media. Pursuit of God's true thoughts frees us from forwarding all the subterfuge of false shepherds in the church who lead the sheep to rebel against authority. Scripture says a man is the way he thinks.[4] This is true of a married couple, also—as they think, so they are.

Don't neglect intimacy in thought, doctrine, and truth. It's hard work, but do it. Everything about your marriage will improve: your discipline of your children, your small talk, your friendships, your emotional intimacy—even your sexual intimacy. The oneness of sexual union is beautiful when it's the fruit of an all-encompassing oneness. Share your thoughts and convictions with your husband or wife. Ask her to share her thoughts with you.

Yesterday, I was talking with a woman recently widowed. Of course, she feels an overwhelming loss and sadness. In our texts and conversations with her, Mary Lee and I have been trying to encourage her for the work she has ahead. As we've talked with her, we've noticed how often she speaks about what her late husband thought about this and that. Not simple stuff like his favorite foods and how much he liked his pickup, but deep stuff like relational difficulties with their children, moral quandaries he faced in his work, and doctrinal matters challenging our congregation (he was an elder).

As an encouragement, I pointed out this intellectual sharing was something she should treasure, giving thanks to God for such a blessing in the years she and her husband had together. I pointed out how many marriages lack such mental intimacy and union, and that she should not take this blessing for granted.

She responded that she had never thought about it, but she and her husband commonly sat together and asked each other, "What are you thinking?" This was a key part of their love habits.

If we're so inclined, we can make many excuses for our lack of mental, intellectual, artistic, aesthetic, ethical, and doctrinal intimacy in our marriage. Our husband is intellectually lazy, caring about nothing but his work, sports, beer, and sex. Our wife is a ninny, caring about nothing but her children, Instagram, videos, and hair. Our husband doesn't appreciate flowers, sunsets, and reading. Our wife doesn't appreciate March Madness, martial arts, and reading. Our husband only reads sports. Our wife only reads Amish romances.

We have our excuses, but we need to be honest about what we really want in our marriage. Do we truly care about our wife or husband? Are we convinced that intimacy in truth, beauty, and goodness between husband and wife is beautiful? Or, more importantly, are we convinced that growing together in our knowledge and commitment to all the truths of God recorded in His Word is the best recipe for joy in this life?

Now then, here are some practical suggestions for growing together as companions emotionally, spiritually, intellectually, and doctrinally.

First, talk about your kids.

When we were dating and first married, Mary Lee and I told each other we would not be one of those couples who

12 SHE IS YOUR COMPANION

only talked about their kids. We have to smile at our conceit back before we had children. Youthful ignorance and pride: we knew it all.

It was only after we had children that we realized it is not only natural, but good, to talk about our children.

Among married couples God has blessed with children, those little ones are a major part of our lives together. Other than God's mercy in Jesus Christ, these little men and women are at the center of what we hold in common. Other people aren't going to want to talk about your children or listen to you talk about them. But you?

You text your husband the funny thing your toddler said that morning and the naughty thing you had to hide your laughter at. When he gets home, the two of you talk about the discipline this or that child needs for this or that sin. You have a school-age daughter struggling with insecurity as she approaches puberty, or an older son in a relationship who needs help. Your daughter off at college needs to decide if she should drop a class so she can better keep up with her other classes. Of course you talk about these things, and why shouldn't you? Children aren't boring and it's not demeaning to your personhood or marriage to think about them together.

As a couple with children, your companionship will often revolve around those children. They are likely to be the most frequent subject of your conversations for many years, even after they themselves marry and have children of their own. Then, moving into a new season of your married life, the conversations of your companionship will expand to include your grandchildren.

Speaking of what to talk about when you're out for dinner, one frequent mistake we made in our earlier years was to bring up difficult subjects then. It might be one of the only times during the week that you have your spouse's undivided attention, so you bring up the touchy subject. You waited until then because the subject is fraught with tension, but as soon as you mention it, the disagreement comes to life and your dinner date is ruined.

So no, you don't want to use your date to hash out the difficult issues. Disagreements you will always have with you, so forget them for the moment and love and enjoy each other.

Talking is good. Communication is imperative to growing in your relationship. If you find yourself struggling with nothing to talk about, consider some friends of ours who used online lists of conversation starters for ideas. Yes, it's weird, but weird can be helpful and good.

Enough about conversation, though. Let's move on to reading together.

Yes, read together. Start before your marriage and keep it up until the end of your life together. Articles and posts are good, but there's no substitute for books. Podcasts are very helpful, but there's no substitute for books. Read books together. Novels, yes—but more importantly, devotional and doctrinal works. Biographies, Christian and otherwise. History.

Major parts of our marital companionship have been changed by me sharing with Mary Lee a passage from a book I was reading. Remember my account back in chapter 7 of how reading Dietrich Bonhoeffer's *Life Together* led us to repent of church-hopping, and to commit ourselves permanently to one church?

Reading together can take different forms. Read the same book, finishing it within a short time of each other, and discuss it. On the other hand, you may want to read aloud to each other (which we struggle to do without falling asleep). Recently, we listened to an audio version of *Moby Dick* while we were driving cross-country. Both the book and listening to it together were great.

Read together, not just for entertainment, but for spiritual growth—especially in repentance. Husband, if some book or article you are reading is good and causes you to reverse your thinking and commitments, go to your wife right away. Strike while the anvil is hot. Read it to her, explaining why you found it helpful and how it has changed your thinking. Explain the changes this truth might mean for your married life. Read it, then talk to her about it. Bring her along with you. Be willing to listen to her challenges when she thinks you are wrong.

Read whenever you can. If you see a chance, take it. Some might call me wacko, but here's just a few of the things I've done to share my life and work with Mary Lee—which in turn have led to us growing together spiritually and doctrinally, becoming better companions for one another. In seminary, I read parts of my textbooks to Mary Lee. Not a whole lot, but anything I was excited about. Parts of Calvin's *Institutes*. Sections of the Westminster Confession of Faith—which, by the way, led to a quite lively conversation late in the evening sitting on our bed. I've shared with Mary Lee large excerpts from Harry Blamires's *The Christian Mind*; chapters from G. K. Chesterton's *Everlasting Man*, *What's Wrong with the World*, *Orthodoxy*, and *The Thing*; Søren Kierkegaard's explosive parables in *Attack Upon Christendom*.

When you have children, if you want them as companions, read to them. Start with *Pat the Bunny* and *Goodnight Moon*, then on to poems. Try the ones by A. A. Milne in *When We Were Very Young*. My own favorite is "Teddy Bear." Mary Lee's favorite is "Lines and Squares." (We both love "The King's Breakfast" and "Disobedience.")

Try out any book by Ralph Moody. He's wonderful and there are few things better for teaching the difference between fatherhood and motherhood. Once our family sat quietly for half an hour in the car, parked in the driveway at the end of a thousand-mile trip home from our family vacation while Mary Lee finished reading us Moody's *Little Britches*. Until it was finished, no one moved.

The list of good books you can choose from is endless.[5]

Of course, Mary Lee and I both had the advantage of mothers who read to us when we were children. Maybe you didn't, but why not start a family tradition yourself?

One of my favorites growing up was the *Polly Pepper* series by Margaret Sidney. Mary Lee's was the *Little House* series by Laura Ingalls Wilder. For some reason, neither of our families ever got into reading Lewis's *Chronicles of Narnia* or Tolkien's *Hobbit* and *The Lord of the Rings*. Countless families, though, have found these favorites, reading them over and over through the years.

Don't miss reading about Bertie and Jeeves in the books by P. G. Wodehouse. James Herriot studied the books by Wodehouse in preparation for writing his own wonderful series based on his practice as a veterinarian in Yorkshire, England. (*All Creatures Great and Small* is the first in the series as published in the US.)

Wonderful memories are formed by reading together as a family. This habit will draw husband and wife closer together as they look forward to the next chapter of the book that evening. Read as a married couple. Read as a family. Read. The couple that reads together grows together.

Here's another thing that helped Mary Lee and me grow in our companionship.

You may be astounded, but for the first fifteen or so years of pastoral ministry, every week I'd come home very late Saturday night, wake Mary Lee up, then read her my sermon for the next morning. From love she would listen, then critique it and make suggestions. She never complained, and several times she told me to start over—which I did.

To this day I can't imagine teaching, writing, or preaching without Mary Lee's criticisms, suggestions, and "I like it." In sixteen years of writing online, rarely has a post been published without being read first to Mary Lee—and it's rare she doesn't change it as I read, making good suggestions for improvement in both tone and substance.

And books? We estimate Mary Lee has heard each chapter of each of my books at least two or three times before the book goes to the editors. (Just now, finishing up this chapter, I read this last part to her and she responded, "True that." Then she took it from me and spent hours working on it.)

Read together. Talk about your reading. Share your thoughts, and watch as the fruit of this work causes you both to grow together—to become better companions.

No matter what work you do as a husband, share that work with your wife. If you're a contractor, share your bidding successes and failures. Share your research of new materials, tools, and work processes. If you're a physician, share your journal articles and read your wife (or husband) the new ethical standards your clinic, healthcare group, or hospital is requiring you to sign. If you're in law school, read and explain the biblical significance of briefs and opinions assigned by your constitutional law prof. If you're in the military, read your wife some of the articles on the difficulties and challenges to Christian consciences posed by being deployed alongside women and the transgendered. If you're a farmer, ask your wife to keep the books, track the federal subsidies, and listen to your thoughts on breeding lines and feed additives.

Marriage is work. Don't be lazy. Marriage never stays the same, but changes with the seasons, years, and decades.

And what you, husband, must remember is that this

change should be guided by you, yet never in a way that patronizes or diminishes or demeans this woman God has given for your wife. If you treat your wife in a condescending way, she will never be Priscilla, you will never be Aquila; and as he preaches, Apollos will remain confused.

Now then, set God's truth at the center of your goal for growth with your wife across the years of your marriage. Listen to Moses' command to the sons of Israel:

> These words, which I am commanding you today, shall be on your heart. You shall teach them diligently to your sons and shall talk of them when you sit in your house and when you walk by the way and when you lie down and when you rise up. You shall bind them as a sign on your hand and they shall be as frontals on your forehead. You shall write them on the doorposts of your house and on your gates.
>
> (Deut. 6:6–9)

We have said a lot about reading. We're sorry to browbeat you about it. That's not our intention, but we are, in fact, people of the Word and the Book, aren't we? And there are so many ways reading and words will help you and your husband or wife to grow in intimacy and companionship.

When your children are young, often there's just not time to fit in anything that doesn't include your children. You take walks together as a family. You play games together. Your reading aloud is from books that children enjoy. All these things are well and good, but as your children get older, the things you can do together will change. Many things you used to do together as a family, you will now be doing as a couple. The things that you were not able to do together now become a possibility.

12 SHE IS YOUR COMPANION

There are different seasons of life, but as you raise your children, remember it's important that your children are not the only thing you have in common. Otherwise, you may wake up one day, empty nesters with nothing in common. If you haven't become companions in anything but childrearing, you might not be able to remember why you ever even liked the person you are sharing a home and bed with. After the kids leave, many marriages fall apart, so work to share common interests. Work to be your wife's or husband's much loved and trusted companion.

One couple we know likes to walk together—not only for the exercise, but also because this is their time together. When it is nice out, they walk in the park. When it's hot, cold, or rainy, they walk the aisles of Menards. They can't fit it in every day, but they do manage several times a week. This is a good time for each of them to catch up with what's going on in the other's life.

Another couple we know likes to cook together. They enjoy having people over for dinner and serving. Not just food, but a delicious meal with beautiful presentation. They enjoy their time together in the kitchen.

One couple we know recently signed up to take an online history class together. It was free and they can watch the class videos at their own pace. The class comes complete with tests that they can decide whether or not to take. If you're generally competitive, you might have fun trying to outdo each other in your grades, but if that is too reminiscent of negative memories from school days, skip the tests.

As your children get older, you might take up a new hobby together. Take a class on cooking, gardening, or genealogy at the local community college. Or skip the class and just learn these things reading books or watching videos online together.

Some things you enjoy doing as a family morph into new phases. If your family has always enjoyed taking hikes, as your children get older, go on backpacking trips or think about a week canoeing in the Boundary Waters.

If your family always enjoyed playing games together, when they are older or gone, you can learn different games involving more strategy. Obviously this does not work for all couples. If one of you tends to be so competitive that you ruin the fun, forget it. And yes, I'll cop to this being true of me—so no, we do not play games together. Our first year of marriage, we gave it up.

Learn to identify the local trees and wildflowers. Take up bird-watching. Take up fishing. Learn about wines and go on winery tours. Learn the constellations. Buy a telescope and visit a planetarium or local observatory. Take a sailing class, buy a sailboat, and regret it. Volunteer at the food kitchen. Visit nursing homes. Go serve missionaries by helping with their carpentry, plumbing, and roof leaks.

There are so many possibilities. Be creative. Do it together and grow closer as companions.

Retired couples have more time and leisure to travel. Go for it. If you used to go camping with your kids, now you can go glamping, rent a camper, or go on a cruise.

For years, friends of ours have enjoyed biking together, but they just entered a new phase of biking by purchasing electric bikes. One of Mary Lee's sisters and her husband enjoy four-wheeling on their back forty in Idaho. (Actually, it's their back hundred thousand owned by Uncle Sam.)

Follow me: healthy marriages are mutual. Not just mutual in bed and on Valentine's Day, but pervasively mutual. It is twisted for a husband and wife to be aloof from one another. Life is togetherness. Intimacy. Fellowship. Friendship. Companionship. Love.

12 SHE IS YOUR COMPANION

How can you dwell in the same house as man and wife while not sharing a single heart beating the tune of your love for one another?

Stop being content with mediocrity. Stop being depressed about your marriage. Stop pretending your marriage is awesome. You're not fooling anyone.

But you can start the hard work of making it so. A marriage of lovers. A marriage of companions.

Conclusion

Unless the Lord Builds the House

Unless the LORD builds the house,
They labor in vain who build it.

— Psalm 127:1

Have you ever built a new house? Mary Lee and I did about twelve years ago. People warned us it would test our marriage: "Couples building a house fight."

Decisions were relentless. Should we put in a heavy foundation that can support a fireplace of solid stone or settle for a lighter foundation that only supports a fireplace of fake stone—or just a veneer? We decided to put in a heavy concrete foundation to support a full stone fireplace, then changed our plans, eventually hiring a mason to cover the hearth with a thin stone veneer. We were left with an overbuilt foundation we'd paid for, and our general contractor reminds us of it, regularly.

How many bathrooms? A deck or just a patio? Which windows? Solid wood or fiberglass doors? Concrete or blacktop driveway? Finished or unfinished basement? Heat pumps or geothermal? Stone or plastic countertops? Light fixtures? Paint colors? On and on it went.

Conclusion UNLESS THE LORD BUILDS THE HOUSE

Building a marriage is like building a house. When you marry, or even before you marry, the decisions are endless, and every decision is critical. Should the groom-to-be ask his intended's father for permission? Is he a Christian? Would he understand your request or would he think his daughter was marrying a freak show? What if he says no? Which pastor should officiate—your own or the pastor of the bride's home church? After the honeymoon, where should you live? Should you use contraception so your wife can finish college, or instead start your family right away?

Making these decisions is hard work. And even after we've made them, we often ask ourselves whether or not we made the right decision. Sometimes we're left wondering, was all that work for nothing?

We all know what it's like to "labor in vain." Back in seminary, I spent a night trying to help my brother David put his rebuilt engine back in in the VW Bug he'd recently bought. We were under his car from late afternoon until 2 AM trying to get the engine lined up with the transmission. It was within less than an inch of seating properly, but that less than an inch didn't yield. Hour after hour. Ten hours of less than an inch until finally, long after we had both given in to complete despair, it seated properly. Ten hours dirty and sweating, lying on the concrete floor pushing and pulling, banging our knuckles, getting irritated with each other, and still failing. Ten hours of laboring in vain.

Marriage, though, is an altogether different thing. Cars come and go. You can mess a car up and you're only out a few thousand dollars. But when you mess up a marriage, you're out a life.

The other day I was visiting a mother of six whose husband just died in his sleep of heart arrhythmia. It was completely unexpected and we're all heartbroken to lose him. But talking about how much she and her children, and the rest of us, miss him, we commented on how awful it is for couples in their fifties and sixties to divorce. Imagine having worked for decades to build your marriage and raise your children, only to throw in the towel near the end of life, returning to singleness and loneliness. How painful for your children and grandchildren to see their parents and grandparents decide all their labors had been in vain, and that they should break apart the home they had built.

Can we understand what could cause a couple in their fifties or sixties to divorce after their children leave home?

If we're honest, yes, we can easily understand this. Marriage is hard work. Of course, it's hard work for you and for your wife or husband. But marriage is hard work for your children also. Your marriage—not theirs—is hard work for them. They grow up seeing and hearing and feeling the conflict, and it's terribly difficult for them because they love their parents. Sometimes they have to speak to us about it. Sometimes they have to rebuke us for our sin against each other—and by extension, our sin against them and their brothers and sisters. Children miss nothing.

After the devastating death of their eldest son (the third of their children who died during childhood), my father and mother moved across the country and began a new life in a new house and community where they were friendless. Dad had to travel a lot, and Mud was left at home raising three younger children, and she often had to do it alone. My older sister had just started at the University of Illinois and was only home for semester breaks. Yet on those breaks, she saw the conflict between Dad and Mud and talked to them about it. She told them they had to stop fighting and get their marriage right—if not for themselves, at least for us younger children. I hadn't known Deborah did this hard work until she told me

CONCLUSION UNLESS THE LORD BUILDS THE HOUSE

recently, but I remember how hard it was living with Dad and Mud in their terrible grief. Things got better. I'm so grateful for the help Deborah gave Dad and Mud.

In their late seventies, Mom and Dad Taylor (Mary Lee's parents) began getting snippy with each other. It was quite noticeable, and after one visit, Mary Lee and I commented on it and decided to pray for them. A year or so later, we visited, and the snippiness was gone. I mentioned to Dad that Mary Lee and I had noticed their impatience with each other and had been praying for them, and that we were happy to see how much better they were with each other. Did he himself think things were better?

He said yes.

Why bring up the difficulties my own and my wife's parents had in their marriages?

Both couples were deeply respected in their church. Both of our fathers were known for their wisdom and leadership. Both were elders of their church. Both couples were thought by most of their friends and acquaintances to have healthy biblical marriages, and they did. Both were healthy biblical marriages. *And* both marriages were hard, filled with disappointments and sin and losses that were hard to sustain across the winters of their unions.

Marriage is hard. Bearing and raising children is hard. Providing for the household is hard. Cooking and cleaning and writing books is hard. I remember my dad's labor on one of his books defining our family prayer times for a year. He got started on the job, then lost interest, but he was under contract to produce the book for a publisher. It had to be finished, so night after night we prayed that Dad would be able to finish that book, and eventually he did.

It seems today Christians feel compelled to lie about their marriages. Especially on social media. I try not to look, but

Mary Lee has to keep up with people's lives so she can help me know what is needed pastorally. Regularly she says to me what lies people tell about their marriage and family life online. One wife would brag about her husband on Facebook, broadcasting to everyone what a godly leader her husband was in their home, and what a great father he was to their children. But my wife was close to this woman. They shared prayer requests, one of which was this same woman asking Mary Lee to pray for her because her husband regularly got drunk and cursed in front of their children. She told Mary Lee her husband was a man "who never denied himself any of his desires." Meanwhile, online, she would brag to all the women of our church how godly and wise and strong and tender and wonderful and awesome her godly, wise, strong, tender, wonderful, awesome husband was.[1]

Every marriage is to a difficult man or woman. The difference between faithful and faithless Christian marriages is not whether or not the marriage is hard, but whether the husband and wife are truthful about it being hard. After all, every marriage is between two sinners, and Scripture is filled with accounts of the sins committed by husbands, wives, sons, and daughters in the homes of God's chosen people. Stop and think about the Patriarchs. King David. King Solomon. The mother of James and John. Ananias and Sapphira.

One way we strengthen ourselves for this hard work is through taking vows. Vows bind us to do something that's typically very right and very hard. The thing we all vowed when we married was "to love and to cherish until death separates us." How easy has that been for you? How easy has that been for your wife?

A couple minutes ago, I was on the phone with my eldest son and told him I'd read 1 Corinthians 13 this morning and

CONCLUSION UNLESS THE LORD BUILDS THE HOUSE

concluded I had no love in me. Have you read it and thought about yourself critically, recently? Let me help:

> Love is patient, love is kind and is not jealous; love does not brag and is not arrogant, does not act unbecomingly; it does not seek its own, is not provoked, does not take into account a wrong suffered, does not rejoice in unrighteousness, but rejoices with the truth; bears all things, believes all things, hopes all things, endures all things.
> Love never fails. (1 Cor. 13:4–8)

But *my* love fails. With my coworkers, elders, the flock we shepherd, my children and grandchildren, my mechanics, neighbors, and the other drivers waiting in line at the light in front of me. But, worst of all, my love fails with the one whom I promised—before God and in the presence of many witnesses—to love and cherish until death. Please pray for me.

One of my many sins is anger. Mary Lee has had to live with this, watching me sin, then shortly after granting me her forgiveness. After a few years of marriage, I despaired of my refusal to put this sin away. I'd sin, then ask forgiveness, then sin, then ask forgiveness, then sin again.

Mary Lee was always quick to forgive me, but it didn't rest easy on my conscience that the sin had such a firm grip on me. One day, after asking her to please forgive me for my anger, I then said, "Lover, I know I have asked you to forgive me for my anger many, many times now. I'm so very sorry, but I know I will soon ask you to forgive me for this again, and it does seem that I'm never repentant and therefore my requests for you to forgive me are insincere. If you think that, I don't blame you. But Lover, what I can say by faith is that God will finish the work He has begun in me, and that includes putting away my sinful anger. So let's pray for it."

Maybe at this point the reader is wondering whether a book on marriage written by a man who confesses his failure to love and cherish his wife could ever be helpful? I respond by asking if there has ever been any other sort of man. (Remember, Jesus wasn't married.) For every husband, marriage is coming face to face with his sins in failing to love and be thankful for the wife God has given him. And the only hope for these sins is that God will persevere with us.

And, true enough, I still sin in anger, but slowly and steadily through the years, this sin has loosened its grip on me, and things have gotten better in our marriage—day by day, month by month, year by year, and decade by decade. In other words, we have pled with God to build our house and He has been faithful to sanctify me. Also to sanctify Mary Lee. Sanctification is a long and painful process, but God has chosen and saved us to holiness—which is always most visible in its absence or presence in the full intimacy of marriage.

Early in marriage, I discovered this verse:

> House and wealth are an inheritance from fathers,
> But a prudent wife is from the LORD. (Prov. 19:14)

How true it was for me. I thought I married a girl who was delightful, lovely, spontaneous, and fun—but God gave me a wife who, besides all of those things, was prudent. How well our Creator knows us, and how kind He is to give us what we don't deserve. And not just a wife, but children too. For Mary Lee and me, five of them. Olive plants all around our table[2] that we couldn't have hoped for. And now, grandchildren also. Twenty-nine so far. A couple times each year, we're able to get together as an entire family, and what joy it is. How much of this I owe to my wife.

For, despite my sins, I do love and cherish Mary Lee.

Conclusion UNLESS THE LORD BUILDS THE HOUSE

Truly. In fact, this book wasn't supposed to be written next. But as I began working on a book for pastors, I thought of how much I love my wife—and it hit me I had faith to write a book on marriage. So here we are. Full of failings and full of sins, and yet able to testify to the Lord's mercy and promises. He has built our house, and I want to help you plead for Him to build yours as well:

> Unless the LORD builds the house,
> They labor in vain who build it.

You can't do it on your own. But if commit your way and trust in Him, He will bring it to pass. If you give yourselves to His church and her love, care, and discipline, you will reap untold benefits. And if you trust God with your sinful marriage, you will have the joy of seeing in it the beauty and glory that God has designed to be a glimpse of the love and joy we look forward to seeing one day at the marriage supper of the Lamb and His Bride. This is our hope, and we trust it will be yours as well. By faith, look for your heavenly Father to bring it to pass:

> Marriage is more than your love for each other. It has a higher dignity and power. For it is God's holy ordinance, by means of which he wills to perpetuate the human race until the end of time. In your love you see your two selves as solitary figures in the world; in marriage you see yourselves as links in the chain of the generations, which God causes to come and go to his glory and calls into his kingdom. In your love you see only the heaven of your bliss, through marriage you are placed at a post of responsibility towards the world and to mankind. Your love is your own private possession; marriage is more than a private affair, it is an estate, an office.

> As the crown makes the king, and not just his determination to rule, so marriage and not just your love for each other makes you husband and wife in the sight of God and man. ... Love comes from you, but marriage from above, from God. As God is infinitely higher than man, so the sanctity, the privilege and promise of love. It is not your love which sustains the marriage, but from now on the marriage that sustains your love.[3]

With all of us, may it be so.

Appendix
Concerning Physical Abuse

Like all other sin, the sin of violence between husbands and wives is present in the church. Christian husbands and wives punch, kick, slap, and choke each other; husbands hit their wives and wives hit their husbands. Husbands initiate the violence sometimes, and other times it is initiated by wives. Sometimes the wife responds to violence violently herself, and sometimes not. Sometimes the husband responds to violence violently himself, and sometimes not.

If you are preparing for marriage, this seems sad, I'm sure. Most couples don't harm one another physically, so rejoice in the unity and love you presently have, but someday you may find yourself unable to deal with conflict in your marriage and home. And tragically, some small number of you may even suffer conflict to the point of violence.

Bear with me then as I discuss the various kinds of violence and how to respond to them. Even if you never need these instructions for your own marriage or home, you'll find them helpful as, in future days and years, you try to come alongside brothers and sisters in Christ committing this sin or suffering under it.

One thing clear in the violence and victims literature, as well as court records and prison statistics, is that the masculinization of women across the Western world has caused a sea change in the number of women committing violent crimes, including domestic violence. Lesbian partners commit it against one another. Wives commit it against their husbands.* Mothers commit it against their children. Here then is an important caution as we look at domestic violence in Christian marriages and families.

During fights, both husbands and wives must be exceedingly careful in their words and actions. Domestic violence is not male only. This is a lie the feminists have promulgated trying to clothe their rebellion against male authority with moral urgency. Of course we all must work together to end the violence; but to justify attacks upon fathers' and husbands'

---

* Sources documenting the above are readily available online. Here's one example: "Life-time prevalence of IPV [intimate partner violence] in LGB [lesbian, gay, and bisexual] couples appeared to be similar to or higher than in heterosexual ones: 61.1% of bisexual women, 43.8% of lesbian women, 37.3% of bisexual men, and 26.0% of homosexual men experienced IPV during their life, while 35.0% of heterosexual women and 29.0% of heterosexual men experienced IPV. When episodes of severe violence were considered, prevalence was similar or higher for LGB adults (bisexual women: 49.3%; lesbian women: 29.4%; homosexual men: 16.4%) compared to heterosexual adults (heterosexual women: 23.6%; heterosexual men: 13.9%)." Luca Rollè, Giulia Giardina, Angela M. Caldarera, Eva Gerino, and Piera Brustia, "When Intimate Partner Violence Meets Same Sex Couples: A Review of Same Sex Intimate Partner Violence," *Frontiers in Psychology* 9 (2018), published August 21, 2018, accessed January 26, 2022, https://doi.org/10.3389/fpsyg.2018.01506; which is citing statistical data from M. L. Walters, J. Chen, and M. J. Breiding, *The National Intimate Partner and Sexual Violence Survey (NISVS): 2010 Findings on Victimization by Sexual Orientation* (Atlanta, GA: National Center for Injury Prevention and Control, Centers for Disease Control and Prevention, 2013).

Appendix Concerning Physical Abuse

authority delegated them by God by claiming that only men commit abuse is a lie from Hell. Yes, everyone believes this lie. Feminists have been incredibly successful in using this to attack God's creation order, but as I said, it's a lie from Hell. Women too commit violence against their intimate partners and children, and women too are moral agents.

As the article cited in the footnote above indicates, when men and women in heterosexual relationships are asked whether they have been the victim of intimate partner violence, 35% of women and 29% of men respond "Yes." That's a gap of only 6%, so we can't continue the charade of speaking and writing warnings against men who abuse while remaining silent about women who abuse.

A husband might sin by saying things demeaning of his wife, and his wife might sin by saying things disrespectful of her husband. A wife might slap her husband, and a husband might slap his wife. Just as there must be no double standard for adultery, there must be no double standard for abuse.

Still, what we call "abuse" must be separated into a couple categories. For instance, once-in-a-lifetime shoving matches, especially when both partners are equally to blame because one initiates and the other immediately retaliates in kind, are cases of violence which should be approached differently than frequent violence perpetrated by only one of the spouses. The first category must be a large warning signal to the husband and wife, and they should confess their sin to their pastor, asking him for help.

Yet not every single, one-off, physical act of anger between husband and wife needs to be confessed to a church authority. There are times when a couple should decide together to seek and grant forgiveness, to pray and confess their sin to God, and then to move on in faith that this one-off will never happen again.

Note well: this does not mean kicking or punching the head, torso, breasts, womb, or genitals; choking; or other forms of serious bodily violence capable of causing permanent injury or death should be left between husband and wife. Nor left between husband, wife, and pastor.

Such serious abuse is subject by God to the civil authority (law enforcement and the courts). Felonies are not the jurisdiction of church officers. Church officers are granted the power of the keys consisting of moral suasion, exclusion from fellowship, and barring the soul from participation in the Lord's Supper. By contrast, God has delegated the sword to the civil authorities, so they are the ones He has placed in jurisdiction over assault and battery, whether inside or outside marriage and family life.

No matter how much the husband or wife wants to hide their spouse's (or child's) sinful assault, they *must* expose it. Absolutely no exceptions. It may feel safer to have the pastor go to the law enforcement officers in your behalf, and that's fine. Allow him or his wife to help you, keeping firmly in mind that God appointed the sword as the means by which the civil magistrate protects life, and this protection begins in the home and between husband and wife.

It is not the elders' or pastor's job to deal with crimes (which is what assault and battery are). Rather, stopping and punishing crimes of violence are the work God Himself has delegated to the civil magistrate He has appointed over you.

If there are circumstances and personalities involved that make it difficult to go to your pastor, see if you can find another church authority and go to them immediately. Otherwise, you must go immediately to your local law enforcement officers.

From very early in pastoral ministry, when Mary Lee and

APPENDIX CONCERNING PHYSICAL ABUSE

I were called in to help in marital conflict, we have understood that abused and battered spouses are often incapable of seeing and evaluating the threat to themselves and their household members presented by a husband or wife who is violent. Violence harms spouses and children—both physically and emotionally.

While writing this section, we heard that a couple who had formerly been members of our church (before moving out of town) recently got in a fight, and the husband beat up his wife. This couple goes to church every week, and no one would have suspected this husband was capable of such a crime against his wife, the mother of his children. They are both professionals, after all.

The police were involved, but it was no surprise to us that the wife refuses to press charges. She says it was not really that bad and she loves him. This is classic, and fortunately, in the state where they live, law enforcement can bring charges even if the wife refuses to do so.

We must remember that crimes of violence in marriage are a serious breach of marital vows. So serious, in fact, that Protestant church officers have long agreed that serious or chronic abuse constitutes abandonment and therefore constitutes biblical grounds for divorce.*

---

* For a helpful discussion of these grounds and surrounding circumstances, see "Divorce and Remarriage," Report of the Ad-Interim Study Committee on Marriage and Divorce to the Twentieth General Assembly of the Presbyterian Church in America, 1992, accessed January 26, 2022, https://pcahistory.org/pca/digest/studies/divorce-remarriage.pdf. The committee writes: "A husband's violence, particularly to the degree that it endangers his wife's safety, if unremedied, seems to us, by any application of Biblical norms, to be as much a ruination of the marriage in fact as adultery or actual departure. This is so precisely because his violence separates them, either by her forced withdrawal from the home or by the profound cleavage between them which the violence produces, as surely as would his own departure, and is thus an expression of his unwillingness 'to consent' to live with her in marriage (1 Cor. 7:12–13; Eph. 5:28–29)."

Furthermore, we must not act as if we don't see indicators of violence in others' marriages. You are your brother and sister's keeper. Step in and help the innocent party recognize his need for outside authority. Yes, it's difficult, but do it. You may well save a life. You may well save the souls of the children.

Endnotes

INTRODUCTION
Your Unique Marriage

1. Leo Tolstoy, *Anna Karenina*, trans. Richard Pevear and Larissa Volokhonsky (2000) (Penguin Books, 2002), 1.

2. Phyllis McGinley, "How Not to Kill Your Husband," ch. 4 in *Sixpence in Her Shoe* (Macmillan, 1964), 30–31.

CHAPTER 1
Till Death

1. G. K. Chesterton, "On Mr. Rudyard Kipling and Making the World Small," ch. 3 in *Heretics* (John Lane Company, 1905), 41.

2. *The Book of Common Prayer: The Texts of 1549, 1559, and 1662*, ed. Brian Cummings (Oxford, 2011), 66.

3. "But I say to the unmarried and to widows that it is good for them if they remain even as I. But if they do not have self-control, let them marry; for it is better to marry than to burn with passion." 1 Corinthians 7:9.

CHAPTER 2
Isaac Was Comforted

1. We dedicated our last book, *Elders Reformed* (Warhorn Media, 2020), to the father.

2. Dorothy Ann Thrupp (attr.), "Savior, like a Shepherd Lead Us," #599 in *Trinity Hymnal*, rev. ed. (Great Commission Publications, 1990), taken from *Hymns for the Young*, 1836.

CHAPTER 3
Male and Female

1. See, for instance, the Met's holding, *Merry Company on a Terrace*, https://www.metmuseum.org/art/collection/search/437749. Or Steen's

The Merry Family on exhibit at Amsterdam's Rijksmuseum, https://www.rijksmuseum.nl/en/collection/SK-C-229.

2. Since God named our race "man" (literally *adam*; Genesis 5:2), we will honor His naming by using "man" to refer to our race inclusive of men and women.

3. Edward Gibbon, *The History of the Decline and Fall of the Roman Empire*, vol. 1 (1776), ed. David Womersley (Penguin Press, 1994), 101n40.

4. See 1 Corinthians 6:9–11.

5. See Charles Murray, *Coming Apart: The State of White America, 1960–2010* (Crown Forum, 2013).

6. Simone de Beauvoir, "Woman as Other," introduction to *The Second Sex*, https://www.marxists.org/reference/subject/ethics/de-beauvoir/2nd-sex/introduction.htm, accessed November 23, 2021.

7. In his comments on Genesis 7:2 (1554), John Calvin explains, "females were added as companions to the males." *Commentary on Genesis*, trans. and ed. John King (1847), The Ages Digital Library Commentary (Books for the Ages, 1998), 176.

8. Some may point out "their" could be referring to society rather than husbands. This seems right, and the point remains.

CHAPTER 4
The Best Wedding Gift

1. "But to think, to speak, is always to exaggerate. By speaking, by thinking, we undertake to clarify things, and that forces us to exacerbate them, dislocate them, schematize them. Every concept is in itself an exaggeration." "In Search of Goethe from Within" in *The Partisan Review* 16, no. 12 (December 1949): 1186.

2. Yes, today there are many brides deployed for combat who are leaving husbands behind, but this is a modern aberration which departs from Scripture's commands and from the beautiful diversity of man and woman as created by God. See "Man's Duty to Protect Woman," Majority Report of the Ad Interim Study Committee on Women in the Military, 2001, presented to the 29th General Assembly of the Presbyterian Church in America, https://www.pcahistory.org/pca/digest/studies/01-278.html.

3. "Now the man called his wife's name Eve because she was the mother of all the living." Genesis 3:20.

CHAPTER 5
What about Birth Control?

See footnotes in chapter.

CHAPTER 6
Leaving and Cleaving

1. Allan Bloom, *The Closing of the American Mind* (Simon & Schuster, 1987), 120–121.

CHAPTER 7
You Need the Church

1. Dietrich Bonhoeffer, *Life Together*, trans. John W. Doberstein (HarperCollins, 1954), 26–28.
2. Cyprian, *On the Unity of the Church* 6, accessed January 21, 2022, https://ccel.org/ccel/cyprian/treatises/anf05.iv.v.i.html.
3. Martin Luther, "Second Christmas Day," sermon, accessed March 7, 2019, http://www.godrules.net/library/luther/129luther_a6.htm.
4. Westminster Confession of Faith, 25.2, https://evangelpresbytery.com/westminster-confession-of-faith/#XXV. See also the Belgic Confession, article 28, https://www.apuritansmind.com/creeds-and-confessions/the-belgic-confession-circa-1561-a-d/.
5. Tim Bayly, *Church Reformed* (Warhorn Media, 2019), 9–10.

CHAPTER 8
Fight the Good Fight

1. Cf. Mark 10:6.
2. A few minutes ago, a member of our church told of one of his friends who has announced he is "transgender" and who said he hoped to be the first recipient of a womb transplant so he could be the first trans person to have an abortion.
3. Charles Hodge, comments on 1 Corinthians 11:19, *An Exposition of the First Epistle to the Corinthians* (Robert Carter & Brothers, 1860), 218.

CHAPTER 9
Labor of Love

1. Readers would benefit from the essay by Dorothy Sayers, "Why Work?"
2. This quotation is taken from the NASB 2020.
3. See Romans 2:4.
4. William Law, *A Serious Call to a Devout and Holy Life* (1729; Christian Classics Ethereal Library), 26, accessed January 25, 2022, https://www.ccel.org/ccel/l/law/serious_call/cache/serious_call.pdf.
5. "I say it bluntly: too many of us American evangelicals are worshipping the bitch goddess of success." Vernon Grounds, "Faith for Failure: A

Meditation on Motivation for Ministry," *TSF Bulletin*, March–April 1986: 4. Grounds borrows the phrase "bitch goddess of success" from American philosopher William James.

6. Calvin Coolidge, "The Press Under a Free Government," an address given to the American Society of Newspaper Editors on January 17, 1925, accessed January 29, 2021, https://www.coolidgefoundation.org/resources/speeches-as-president-1923-1929-16/.

7. "Therefore, consider the members of your earthly body as dead to immorality, impurity, passion, evil desire, and greed, which amounts to idolatry." Colossians 3:5.

8. The full charge is available at http://baylyblog.com/blog/2006/07/ordination-charge-son.

9. See Titus 2:3–5.

10. See also Deuteronomy 18:4; 26:1–12; Leviticus 27:26; etc.

CHAPTER 10
One Flesh

1. "Keeping of stews" was the phrase commonly used in the sixteenth century to refer to what we now call houses of prostitution, massage parlors, and bathhouses.

2. The Westminster Larger Catechism (1647), accessed January 26, 2022, https://evangelpresbytery.com/westminster-larger-catechism/.

3. Though it's not much used today, this word has a long history in theological and pastoral contexts. It refers to a burning desire, especially a sexual one. It's perhaps most familiar from Augustine's *Confessions*, where the word sums up for him his difficulty controlling his urges as an unbelieving young man.

4. Martin Luther on "Thou shalt not commit adultery," identified as the Sixth Commandment (per Roman Catholic and Lutheran tradition) in *The Large Catechism*, trans. F. Bente and W. H. T. Dau, in *Triglot Concordia* (Concordia Publishing House, 1921), 643.

CHAPTER 11
Raising Children

1. See Romans 5:12–21; 1 Corinthians 15:20–21.

2. This quote is commonly, though apparently falsely, attributed to Francis of Assisi. See Glenn Station, "FactChecker: Misquoting Francis of Assisi," The Gospel Coalition, July 10, 2012, accessed February 3, 2022, https://www.thegospelcoalition.org/article/factchecker-misquoting-francis-of-assisi/.

3. *Daddy Tried* (Warhorn Media, 2016).

4. In several places, Scripture matter-of-factly acknowledges a woman to be "beautiful of form and face" (e.g., Genesis 29:17; Esther 2:7), and it's not lustful for the Holy Spirit to do so.

5. Romans 16:16; 1 Corinthians 16:20; 2 Corinthians 13:12; 1 Thessalonians 5:26.

CHAPTER 12
She Is Your Companion

1. Calvin, commentary on Acts 18:26 (1552), trans. Christopher Fetherstone (1585), ed. Henry Beveridge, in *Commentary on the Acts of the Apostles*, The Ages Digital Library Commentary (Books for the Ages, 1998), 628.

2. For example, in his Acts commentary (commended by Charles Spurgeon), nineteenth-century Anglican F. C. Cook wrote: "Priscilla appears to have been endowed largely with those spiritual gifts which are bestowed on eminent believers for the good of the Church. Without taking any public part in the ministrations of the Church, which would have been contrary to apostolic discipline (see 1 Corinthians 14:34), she was able to speak convincingly to the heart on all suitable occasions, and it may be on account of that gift that she is even named before Aquila in more than one passage of Holy Writ." F. C. Cook, *The Acts of the Apostles*, new edition (Longmans, Green, and Co., 1866), 227. Likewise, pastor of Westminster Chapel in London, G. Campbell Morgan, wrote in his Acts commentary: "There were two people in Ephesus who knew much more about Jesus than [Apollos] did: a woman and a man. The order of the names is significant, 'Priscilla and Aquila.'" G. Campbell Morgan, *The Acts of the Apostles* (Fleming H. Revell Co., 1924), 440.

3. Westminster Confession of Faith, 24.2, https://evangelpresbytery.com/westminster-confession-of-faith/#XXIV.

4. "For as he thinks within himself, so he is." Proverbs 23:7.

5. Here's a great list put together by our eldest, Heather Ummel: https://warhornmedia.com/reading-with-children.

CONCLUSION
Unless the Lord Builds the House

1. Yes, our elders were involved, and finally the family rejected the elders' discipline and left the church.

2. "Your wife shall be like a fruitful vine / Within your house, / Your children like olive plants / Around your table. / Behold, for thus shall the man be blessed / Who fears the LORD." Psalm 128:3–4.

3. Dietrich Bonhoeffer, "A Wedding Sermon from a Prison Cell," in *Prisoner for God: Letters and Papers from Prison*, ed. Eberhard Bethge, trans. Reginald H. Fuller (Macmillan, 1953, 1959), 35–36.

Scripture Index

Genesis
- 1:31 11
- 1:26–28 108
- 2:15 . . . . . 11, 108
- 2:18–25 168
- 2:23 . . . . .11–12, 36
- 2:24 . . . . . 16, 67
- 7:2 36
- 17:7 157
- 24:16 21
- 24:63–66 21
- 24:67 21
- 38:6–10 . . . . 49ff.
- 45:14 153
- 46:29 153

Exodus
- 20:8–10 115
- 22:29–30 122
- 34:26 122

Numbers
- 30:1–2 15

Deuteronomy
- 4:40 157
- 6:6–9 . . . 145, 176
- 6:10–12 111–111
- 24:5 42

1 Samuel
- 20:41 154

Job
- 5:7 143

Psalm
- 51:5 143–144
- 51:14 58
- 100:3 28
- 127:1 . . . . . 180ff.
- 127:3 49
- 127:4–5 143

Proverbs
- 1:5 105
- 4:23 140
- 6:27–29 136
- 12:15 105
- 14:23 109
- 19:14 186
- 22:6 . . . . . 4, 158

Proverbs (cont'd)

27:9 105
30:8–9 111

Ecclesiastes

5:19 116

Isaiah

54:13 158
65:19, 21–22 . . .108

Jeremiah

17:9 146

Hosea

1:2–3 139

Malachi

2:14 162
2:15 63

Matthew

5:27–29 137
5:45 109
6:14–15 85
6:19–21 63
6:24 . . . . 62, 112
12:48–50 70
13:22 112
19:4 . . . . . 28, 101
19:6 11
19:16–23 . . . . 62ff.
22:35–40 . . 133–133
23:37–38 . . 159–159

Mark

10:6 27
10:6–8 76
10:13–15 64
10:13–16 . . . 146ff.

Luke

12:7 5

John

7:24 112
8:31–32 169
13:23–25 154
13:34 154

Acts

2:39–40 158
16:31 158
18:3 162
18:24–26 . . .162ff.
20:37–38 154

Romans

1:26 36
9:21 67
12:2 3
13:1–2 35
16:3–5 164

1 Corinthians

7:3–4 . . . . . .128ff.
7:4 141
11:7–9 34
11:19 106

1 Corinthians (cont'd)
13:4–8 185

2 Corinthians
1:3–4 18

Galatians
4:26 . . . . . . 77ff.

Ephesians
4:26 . . . . . . 87ff.
4:28 116
5:22–24 37
5:25–28 37
5:28–32 140

Colossians
3:5 112
3:19 38
3:21 40
3:23–24 107

2 Thessalonians
3:10 . . . . . . 96, 115

1 Timothy
2:12–15 32
5:1–2 141

Titus
3:14 117

Hebrews
12:14 83
13:4 124
13:5 112

James
1:8 146

1 Peter
3:1 37
3:7 . . . . . . 38, 132

1 John
5:3 134

Printed by Libri Plureos GmbH in Hamburg, Germany